IN THE GERMAN MILLS OF DEATH

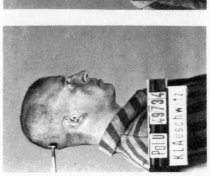

The author on arriving in the concentration camp at Auschwitz, July 1942.

IN THE
GERMAN
MILLS OF DEATH

1941-1945

PETRO MIRCHUK

THE SURVIVORS OF THE HOLOCAUST
Washington, New York, London, Munich

Published by Vantage Press, Inc.,
516 West 34th St., New York, New York 10001

Standard Book Number 533-01908-7

SECOND EDITION
1985

Published by the Survivors of the Holocaust
and
the Ukrainian American Freedom Foundation, Inc.,
345 Carter Street, Rochester, N.Y. 14621, USA.

Printed in the United Kingdom by Ukrainian Publishers Ltd.
200, Liverpool Road, London, N1 1LF

CONTENTS

INTRODUCTION

I am a Ukrainian. Whenever I mention that during World War II, from 1941 until the end of the war in May, 1945, I was a prisoner of the German concentration camp at Auschwitz, I am never believed.

"You mean that you are a Ukrainian Jew? How could you, a Ukrainian, be sent to a German concentration camp? It is known that the Ukrainians cooperated with the Germans. When the Germans entered the Ukraine, the Ukrainian population greeted them with flowers."

This disbelief is why I find it necessary to give a brief introduction to my memoirs of my experiences in a Nazi concentration camp.

First, the generally accepted belief that only Jews were imprisoned and annihilated in the concentration camp at Auschwitz is incorrect. As a matter of fact, in addition to about three million Jewish victims, there were in Auschwitz about one-half million non-Jewish prisoners. Among these latter were the Ukrainians.

Second, while it is true that the German army was greeted with flowers when it entered Ukraine, to assume that this was done because the Ukrainians were Nazi sympathizers or wished to cooperate with the German government is to be either ignorant of the situation or anti-Ukrainian.

The true reasons for this demonstration are absolutely different. In order to understand these reasons, it is necessary to know the political situation in which the Ukrainian population lived on the eve of World War II.

At the end of World War I, when in February, 1917 the

Revolution broke out in Russia, Ukraine[1] declared its independence. In western Ukraine, then occupied by Austria, independence was declared in September, 1918. On January 22, 1919, both parts united to form the Ukrainian National Republic. The newly formed independent state was immediately involved in a difficult three-front war against the White Russian Army, the Bolshevist Army, and the Polish Army. After three years of fighting, the war for independence was lost, and Ukraine was immediately divided into four parts. The largest part, the eastern and central sections, had a population of thirty million and was occupied by Red Russia. The western part, with a populartion of ten million, was occupied by Poland. A small section of one-half million population came under Rumanian rule. The remainder, containing another one-half million people, was joined to the Czechoslovakian republic.

Life under the Russian occupation was extremely hard. Bloody executions took place not only immediately after the fighting, but later, too. The infamous Red Russian Cheka[2] applied extremely cruel mass terror against all those who, in their opinion, were dangerous to the Russian occupation.

From 1923 to 1928 was the period called "Ukrainization." During this period, the government of Communist Russia still didn't feel strong enough to maintain total control and, therefore, pretended to respect the national rights of the Socialist Republics. The Ukrainians were permitted to organize Ukrainian schools, publish Ukrainian literature, and so on, but this freedom lasted only a short time. The purpose in allowing this was so that the occupation government could find out who

[1]"Ukraine": The use of an article is generally accepted with this name, i.e., "the Ukraine." However, this is strongly opposed by Ukrainians, since the addition of an article to the name of a country implies that it is a part of another nation or state, which Ukraine is not. Accordingly, we use only the form "Ukraine" here and never "the Ukraine."

[2]"Cheka," or "Che-Ka": This is the abbreviation of the first Russian Communist political police—Chreswychayna Komisiya meaning special commision—responsible for unspeakable terror during the "Civil War." The Report of the Cheka of All Russia for the first two years of its existence gives cold figures: 1,700,000 persons executed during these two years, according to B. Kamyshansky in I Am a Cossack. Especially bloody terror was applied by the Cheka in occupied Ukraine.

believed in and worked for an independent Ukraine. At the end of the 1920s and the beginning of the 1930s, Ukrainian writers, university professors, and hundreds of other members of the "intelligentsia" were imprisoned; most of them were liquidated in the prisons without any trial, while others were brought for special "monster trials," sentenced as "enemies of the people," and sent to Siberia.

In 1932-33, in order to break the resistance of the Ukrainian farmers, Stalin ordered the organization of an artificial famine. In the fall of 1932 all corn was taken by force from the peasants, collected in special places, and sent to Moscow. The peasants were told that the corn would be divided according to "social justice" to everyone in Ukraine, but in reality Stalin had something else entirely in mind. The peasants received almost nothing back.

In the spring of 1933 a horrible famine broke out. After Stalin had died and Khrushchev talked openly about the famine for the first time, he admitted that during that terrible time, at least four to six million Ukrainians died from starvation. Whole families died. Whole villages died. Khrushchev mentioned that he personally knew of cases where mothers, crazy from hunger, ate their children. This kind of mass terror from Soviet Russia continued until World War II.

In the section occupied by Poland the situation was a little better. There was not such a total terror applied against the Ukrainian population, but, nevertheless, all Ukrainian national life was suppressed; educated Ukrainians, and even peasants, who wanted to read a Ukrainian book or have a Ukrainian press were persecuted and put into prison.

This is why the Ukrainian people were eager for a war. A new world war was their only hope that their unbearable situation could be changed. All Ukrainians felt that whoever might come into Ukraine would fight against Poland and Soviet Russia, and any enemy of Russia would be a friend to Ukrainians. Whoever came would liberate them from the horrible situation they were enduring.

The greatest hope of the Ukrainians rested with Germany. The Polish and Russian presses reported that the Germans were fighting for the rights taken away from them at the end of World War I. The effect of the knowledge that the

Germans were fighting for their rights was that the Ukrainians thought that the Germans would respect the rights of other nations and other peoples. This feeling was especially widespread because, in Europe, Germany was thought of as the center of modern western civilization and culture. No one at that time suspected that the Germans were capable of doing the same things the Red Russians had done.

Therefore, when, in June, 1941, the German Army entered Ukraine, it was greeted with flowers as the liberator. The Germans were expected to crush the Russians and help the Ukrainians restore a free life and independent Ukrainian state.

At the end of the war, when all documents and protocols of the Nazis were revealed, it became known that Germany, when it entered the war against Russia, did not intend to liberate Ukraine and other countries of eastern Europe, but, on the contrary, Hitler planned to occupy Ukraine and make it a German colony. The Ukrainian people were to be used as slaves to help in the rebuilding of destroyed German territory and then would have been sent to Siberia. The Ukrainian territory was to have been used as an area for German colonization. Those plans were totally suppressed at the time. Even the German leaders never talked about them among themselves.

It was for these reasons, then, that the Ukrainians greeted the German Army with flowers.

The Nazis soon demonstrated what they were looking for in Ukraine, and this changed the friendly attitude of the Ukrainian people into passive hostility and active resistance overnight. Flowers were soon replaced with weapons.

IN THE GERMAN MILLS OF DEATH

Chapter 1

ON THE EVE

The outbreak of the German-Polish war on September 1, 1939, found me in the Polish prison at Lvov,[1] capital of western Ukraine.

In the period between 1932, when I finished my high school education, and 1939, I was put into prison six times by the Polish police as a suspected member of the Ukrainian underground movement. Fortunately enough, each time I was released because the police were not able to collect evidence of my activities in the underground.

This time I was in prison with about one hundred other Ukrainian students arrested by Polish police in March, 1939 during a conference of the Ukrainian Students' Organization.

At that time we were permitted to have local organizations of Ukrainian students, but we were not allowed to have a central organization. As a result, we had legal local Ukrainian students' organizations and an illegal central organization.

In 1939 a conference of this illegal organization was held and, about five minutes before the end of the conference,

[1]"Lvov": This is the Ukrainian spelling of the capital of Western Ukraine. It is written as "Lwów" in Polish, "Lvov" in Russian, and "Lemberg" in German. In order not to confuse the American reader, we use the form accepted in English, "Lvov." The same applies to other geographical names—for instance, the river "Bug," which is 'Buh" in Ukrainian.

some one hundred Polish policemen with clubs and guns broke through both doors of the house where the conference was being held and entered the room. We were ordered to put our hands up and turn our faces to the wall. Everyone was searched and severely beaten. Then we were brought out of the house and thrown into cars. The cars took us to prison where we were interrogated at length. We remained in prison until September, 1939 when war broke out between Germany and Poland.

Ten days after the start of the war, the German Army reached the outskirts of Lvov. The Polish Army in Lvov continued to fight, but a few days later, the Russian Army entered Poland from the east and reached Lvov from the eastern part. In the last moments immediately after the capitulation of the Polish Army and before the Russian Army entered Lvov, all prisoners were released. From a Ukrainian priest who was the chaplain for the Ukrainian soldiers in the Polish Army, we learned that there was an agreement between Russia and Germany, the so-called "Molotov Pact." According to its terms, Russia was to occupy the whole western part of Ukraine up to the Sian and Bug Rivers. The territory west of this line was to become a part of Germany.

It was extremely dangerous for Ukrainian nationalists to wait for the Russian occupation. We all knew of the experiences of the eastern Ukrainians. Had we remained, we knew we would soon have been imprisoned once again by the Russians and liquidated. Therefore, we had to escape, to go into exile in the west as soon as possible.

I immediately crossed the Sian River into the territory occupied by Germany. Just west of the Sian-Bug line there was a small strip of territory where about one-half million Ukrainians lived. Here I started to work in a Ukrainian youth organization.

While I had been in the gymnasium, which corresponds to the American elementary and high schools, I had had seven years of study in German. Therefore, I was now able to speak German with the German authorities. Of course, I expected to meet representatives of the founders of western European civilization. I was quickly disenchanted.

One day, in a small town near the Russian-German

boundary, I saw something unusual. There was a large crowd of people surrounded by German soldiers with dogs. The soldiers were forcing the people, by beating and kicking, to move toward the river that now separated Russia and Germany. I was told that the people were the Jews who lived in this section. The Gestapo had ordered them all together—men, women and children—and was trying to force them to cross the river into Russia. They were all horrified by the dogs, especially the children, and many were crying. The dogs jumped and bit at them, and when someone fell down, he was kicked by the soldiers until he stood up and walked again. It was very cruel and inhuman. It was not the treatment I had expected from the Germans.

The Jewish people were finally brought to the river. When they saw the other side, they began to shout, "Long live Stalin!" Unfortunately for them, the Russian police were waiting with their guns and denied them entrance into the territory. They were forced back. The shouting of "Long live Stalin!" was replaced with "Long live Hitler!" But it didn't help.

After about an hour of running back and forth in the river, the Jews were permitted to come back into the German section. The police put them into lines and took them to a special camp outside the town.

I was never a "Jewish uncle," but I was also never anti-Semitic. Such cruel torturing of people, especially of women and children, horrified me. Since I could speak German, I went to the *Ortskommando*, the place of the German command, and tried to express my opinion that this was a terrible thing, and that it would prove to be a very unpopular thing for the German government. The chief of police, an extremely unfriendly man, asked me who I was. When I explained that I was a Ukrainian political refugee who had escaped from a Polish prison and had fled the Russian persecution to Germany hoping to find freedom, he told me that I was lucky that I was Ukrainian. He told me that otherwise I would have been put in the special camp with the Jewish people, or even executed immediately. He warned me to never interfere with Germans, and to leave that section immediately.

After meeting with other Ukrainians who had already had

some experience with the Germans and who knew the situation, I decided to leave for another section.

After I moved, I continued to work in a Ukrainian youth organization, and soon came into conflict with the Germans again.

This time in Kniazhpil, a village near Bilgoraj inhabited half by Ukrainians and half by Poles, a German soldier met a Polish girl. When she fled to her house, he followed. Showing his gun, he forced the girl's mother and younger sister to remain in the house. In their presence he raped the girl, then forced the mother to clean the girl's blood off his pants. The incident soon became known to the whole village, and everyone was enraged.

I thought that as a foreigner I would be permitted to report to the German command and explain to them that such an incident should not be allowed. So again I went to the *ortskommandant* with the same result as before. He told me to leave the section immediately, and that only because I was a political refugee was I not executed.

Again I moved, this time to Krakow. From there I went to Prague, Czechoslovakia.

In Prague there was a Ukrainian university, organized and supported by the Czechoslovakian government before the German occupation. The university continued to function under German rule.

I was accepted at the university and was permitted by the Germans to continue my law studies under the condition that I would, at the same time, be a student at the German Carl's University in Prague.

In 1941 I completed my law studies from both universities and received my doctorate of law from the Ukrainian university in June.

I was to receive my doctor's degree at the German Carl's University in December, but it never came to that. When I was a student in Prague I had started publishing a Ukrainian monthly in which I advocated the equality and freedom of all nations. As I later found out, this was contrary to the ideology of Hitler's National Socialism. Therefore, after two issues were published, I was arrested and interrogated by the German Secret Police. Fortunately for me, there was a *Volks-*

deutsch, a German born and raised in the Ukraine, working there. After the interrogation, he warned me that I would be arrested in connection with the publication of my bulletin. It was the end of the academic year and only the ceremony of receiving the diploma of academic degree remained, so, since I had been warned not to attend the ceremony, I left Prague and went to Vienna.

At that time there were already evident differences in the offical political attitudes of Hitler's NSDAP on one side and the members of the Headquarters of the German Army, and especially the *Abwehr*, the counterintelligence unit headed by Admiral Canaris, on the other side.

A Ukrainian political leader in exile knew of these differences and he and the leadership of an organization to which I belonged took advantage of them. In cooperation with the command of the German Army, they organized a Ukrainian Legion, a detachment of the future Ukrainian Army, which was to fight against Russia. It was evident that war against Russia was imminent, and the German Army was interested in having the support and cooperation of the people of the territory the German Army had to enter.

After I completed my studies, I came to Vienna as liaison officer to the *Oberkommando der Wehrmacht*, the OKW, the Head Command of the German Army. Of course, since the Gestapo was still looking for me, it was necessary to change my name, but that was no problem for the OKW. I immediately received a passport under the assumed name of Herr Peter von Gutenfeld. For two months I stayed in Vienna.

In June, when Germany attacked Russia, there was an uprising in Ukraine, the reestablishment of the independent Ukraine was proclaimed, and a Ukrainian government was formed.

It was interesting to find out what the reaction of the German leadership would be to this act. Very soon the answer came. Stepan Bandera, the leader of the Ukrainian liberation movement (OUN), and the Prime Minister of the new Ukrainian government were invited by a representative of the German government to discuss the problems created by the presence of the German Army in Ukraine. During this meeting, Bandera and the Prime Minister were arrested and imprisoned. Nevertheless, I wanted to go to Ukraine and to see personally what was happening there.

In the middle of August I left Vienna and returned to Lvov. There I started to work in the Institute of Education which had replaced the old Department of Education. For two days I visited in the place where my family—my parents and brothers and sisters—lived, about thirty miles from Lvov. I intended to return for a longer visit in October but, on September 15, three Gestapo agents entered my office in the Institute. They told me to put my hands up, but were momentarily confused by my German suit. (While I was in Vienna I had bought a German suit and was now wearing it.) They took my identity card and, seeing the name von Gutenfeld, they told me to leave immediately because this was a Gestapo action.

Unfortunately there was with the Gestapo agents a *Volksdeutsch* whom I had known personally, and he told them that my identity card was false and gave them my real name. Once again I had to put my hands up and face the wall. This time they checked all the papers in my desk and found not only my real identity card, but also another false card. This I had intended to use to go farther east. It was made out in the name of Mr. Ivanenko. The Gestapo officer remarked sarcastically that he had captured three men: Herr von Gutenfeld, Dr. Mirchuk, and Mr. Ivanenko. I was put in a police car with all the others working in my office and taken to the police prison at Loncki Street. So, after two years, I was back in the same prison where, in the spring of 1939, I had been brought by the Polish police, the known arch-enemies of Ukrainian patriots. This time I had been brought by a rep esentative of the German nation, the people we had regarded as friends and had expected to support us in our fight for freedom against Russia.

All the rooms of the prison were overcrowded. There had been massive arrests of Jews and leaders of the Ukrainian nationalist movement. When I was being taken across the backyard of the prison, I saw many Ukrainian girls who had been arrested in the wake of this massive action standing in front of the wall with their hands up. Among them were my two sisters who had just come to Lvov to visit me and who were caught in the building where I worked.

After I was registered by a police clerk, I asked if they would return the money confiscated from me during my arrest to my sisters because they would need it to return home. He laughingly refused my request.

There were so many people in each room that it was impossible to sit on the floor. We were left in these cramped quarters and received nothing to eat except some water at midday. The police officers would not permit anyone to leave the rooms to go to the toilet, so many were forced to urinate right in the room and the stench was horrible.

We were forbidden to look out the window, and if the police saw a face in the window they would start shooting. Nevertheless, we managed to look out occasionally and found that the girls who had been arrested with us, after standing by the wall for about five or six hours with their hands up, had been released.

When evening came we received some soup for our supper, then were ordered to sleep. Of course, in the crowded rooms, no one was able to lie down. There was no room for that. Sleep was impossible.

In the morning a new transport of prisoners was brought in. There was no room for them in the cells, so they were put in the corridors. From these new prisoners we got the information that the Gestapo had planned the same action on the same day, September 15, in all cities in western Ukraine. In all these cities the leaders of the Ukraine underground movement were arrested by the Gestapo. Some had been transported here, but since the prison was so overcrowded, the rest were waiting in prisons in other towns.

In the morning of our third day in prison, some prisoners were taken from the cells, put in big trucks, and taken away from the prison. We speculated for about three hours about what was happening, then one of our friends who had been taken was returned to the corridor. He told us that the Gestapo was taking groups of Jewish prisoners outside the town and executing them. Among the Jewish prisoners were some Ukrainians. One of the Ukrainians was blond with blue eyes and a policeman noticed him and asked how he could be a Jew when he looked like a German. When the prisoner told him he was not a Jew, but a Ukrainian, the policeman asked the Gestapo why the Ukrainians were being executed with the Jews. The execution was stopped, the Ukrainians were ordered back into the truck and were brought back to the prison. This incident let us know that we were not yet to be executed, but left us wondering what the future held for us. We decided that probably we would be executed after the last of the Jewish prisoners.

In my room there were only Ukrainian prisoners, all members of the underground movement and well known to each other. We discussed the situation among ourselves and decided that if we were brought up for execution we would have to fight. We would try to jump from the truck and take guns from the Gestapo.

After three days, our group of about two hundred Ukrainians was taken from the prison, placed in trucks, and taken from the town. No one knew what was happening, so we prepared ourselves to fight before being executed. However, we soon saw that we had passed the place of execution. Several hours later we came to another town and were taken to a prison and ordered out of the trucks. When we got out we found that we had been brought to the Polish prison Montelupich in Krakow.

Here our situation was a little better. In our cell, intended for two persons, six were placed. Of course it was still crowded, but compared to the rooms we were in at Lvov, it was very comfortable. There was no room for beds, so we all had to sleep on the floor. They gave us blankets and pallets to be shared by two prisoners. So we slept in relative comfort.

For the next six weeks we were not permitted to leave our cells, nor were we permitted to shave or wash. We received black coffee in the morning and we would drink half of it and save the other half for washing. Once a week we collected the coffee for washing our shirts.

Conditions at the prison were hard. In a few weeks everyone—unshaven, dirty, and long-haired—looked like present-day hippies. We received 150 grams of bread in the morning, a quart of soup for lunch, and one-half quart of coffee for supper.

We were registered as Ukrainians and were not permitted

to write letters. The Polish prisoners had been in prison long enough to have an organized Red Cross. A representative of the Polish Red Cross came regularly once a week, took letters from the prisoners to their families, and gave them small packages.

Nevertheless, we felt better because we knew there was no immediate danger of execution. Had the Gestapo intended to execute us right away, they would have taken us to a suburb of Lvov rather than bring us hundreds of miles to a Polish prison in Krakow.

In the morning, and before going to sleep, there was a roll call. We all had to stand in a line and each had to report how many were in the cell. After roll call was completed, we were permitted to pray. We convinced our guard that it was a Ukrainian custom to sing the prayer. In that way we could keep track of our friends in other cells. If we could hear them singing, we knew they were still there.

Life in the cell was very monotonous; there was nothing to do. We were ordered only to clean the floor and the urinal bucket. Each floor had only one toilet and each cell had a urinal bucket. In the morning we had to take the bucket to the toilet and empty it, then bring it back to the room and clean the outside of it.

One day, when I was bringing the bucket to the toilet, I saw an empty paper box in the corridor. I put it inside the bucket and took it into my room. With a great deal of difficulty I stole a pencil from the guard and when we got the soup we managed to keep one of the spoons. From the spoon we made a knife and then I cut the paper box into pieces and made a set of cards. During the days I was making the cards, the others wondered what the reason was for making cards since we were all waiting to be executed or sent to a concentration camp. Psychologically we were not prepared to play cards. However, when the cards were finished and I had explained the rules of bridge, everyone wanted to play. So every day after we had cleared the floor and the bucket, we started to play bridge. We played until lunch and then again until supper. The whole day was filled in that way with card-playing.

After six weeks, the Gestapo began interrogating the

Ukrainian prisoners. During the interrogations, one of the prisoners told the Gestapo that he had been imprisoned totally by accident. He said that he was working on the railroad and that since the mail was then so poorly organized, a friend had asked him to deliver a letter when he was in Lvov. While he was delivering the letter, the Gestapo were arresting Ukrainians in the office he had brought the letter to and he was arrested by mistake along with the others. He also told them that as far as he knew, he was German on his mother's side, and couldn't understand why he had been arrested. The Gestapo checked his story and found that he had had nothing to do with the underground movement. He was released from prison and taken to a Ukrainian committee in Krakow so that he could get help in getting back to Ukraine. His release provided an opportunity for us to send the Ukrainian committee information about our location. Because of this information the committee organized a Ukrainian Red Cross. It was accepted by the German administration, so, in addition to the Polish Red Cross, the Ukrainian Red Cross also worked in Montelupich Prison in Krakow. Now we were permitted to write a letter to our families once a month and to receive a package each week from the Ukrainian Red Cross.

We had already had good experiences the previous times we were in Polish prisons, so we now exploited the delivery of packages by the Red Cross for organizing a way to mail additional letters secretly. When the truck from the Ukrainian Red Cross with the packages came to the backyard of the prison, one of the prisoners helping with the unloading gave one of his packages to the police guard as a gift. While the guard was looking for a place to hide the package, the prisoner would place an envelope containing our secret mail in the truck and take from it the mail for us. In that way we could inform our families and friends about our situation and receive much more information than was possible through the regular mail which was, of course, carefully censored by the Gestapo.

The man who had been freed had been in my room. After his release, another was brought to replace him. The new prisoner was not a Ukrainian political prisoner. He was a criminal, and we were not sure if he were really a prisoner or perhaps a Gestapo agent. We were very careful with our discussions in his presence, but in a way he helped us kill the boredom of the prison. When he saw that we were playing cards using very simple pieces of old paper, he told us that he would bring us a set of real cards. One day, when he took the buckets to the toilet, he managed to steal a deck of cards from a guard. Now we could play with real cards.

In the door there was a small opening we prisoners called a "Judas." Through this "Judas" a guard could look into the cell from time to time to check on what we were doing. Of course, we always tried to hide what we were doing by having a prisoner stand in front of the "Judas" to block the guard's vision, but it was not always possible to do this.

A few days after the new prisoner got us the deck of cards, one of the guards saw that we were playing with a real deck. He ordered us to open the door and go out into the corridor. He searched us all carefully, then searched the room. He found nothing. We went back into the room and continued our card game.

The guard could not understand why he had been unable to find the cards, so he called ten other guards. We were once more ordered into the corridor and searched thoroughly. Again they found nothing. After returning to the cell, we continued to play, and the criminal who was with us was thoroughly enjoying the situation.

The guards tried many more times to catch the cards, but in vain. They never found out how it was possible that they were unable to find them. Only the prisoners in our cell knew what was going on.

The secret was that the criminal was a professional pickpocket. So when we heard the key being put in the door, we quickly gave all the cards to him. As we went out into the corridor, he slipped the cards into the pocket of a guard. After the search was completed and nothing was found, we would be ordered to return to the cell. On our way back in the thief would remove the cards from the guard's pocket, and we would happily continue our game.

Beside Polish and Ukrainian prisoners, there were many Jewish prisoners as well. There was a difference in their treatment, however. Polish and Ukrainian prisoners were interrogated about the activities and movements of the underground. The Jewish prisoners were not interrogated. They had been brought here only to await transport to the concentration camp in Auschwitz. They stayed in this prison for only a few days or sometimes a few weeks.

Through the window in our cell we had opportunities to see the sadistic "games" in which the Gestapo forced these Jewish prisoners to participate. One of the games was what the Gestapo called "Building Pyramids." A group of Jewish prisoners was brought into the backyard of the prison and ordered to march in a circle. While they marched they had to sing a Polish song saying that the Jewish people did not have to work when there was a Polish premier, Rydz-Smigly, but that when Hitler came to power he taught the Jews to work. After they finished the song, they were ordered to build pyramids. They had to bring hot charcoal from the kitchen in their bare hands to build the pyramids. The extreme pain caused by the burning coals brought about a great deal of crying, and when one fell down he was shot by a Gestapo agent and another was ordered to take his place.

Another "game" was called "Masonry," and was supposed to teach a Jew to be a mason. For this game, individual prisoners were singled out and brought into the prison's backyard. The prisoner was forced to climb a ladder onto the top of the building. He was then to pretend to paint or build. If the prisoner hesitated while he was climbing the ladder, he was shot, so many tried to hurry up onto the roof, but even this didn't help. Once on the roof, the prisoner served as a target for Gestapo shooting practice and had to remain there until he was shot and fell off.

Another of these sadistic activities involved bringing a group of Jewish prisoners to the cesspool located in the backyard of the prison. They were ordered to undress, get into the pool, and empty it with their hands into buckets. When the buckets were filled, the prisoners had to carry them into the prison and empty them in the toilets. They continued this until they were exhausted and fell into the cesspool and drowned.

Almost every morning a group of prisoners was called out by names and taken away. Before they were taken away, they were told to take off their shoes. Later we found out that the prisoners who had to take off their shoes were marked for execution. There was a shortage of shoes in wartime Germany and therefore the Gestapo always collected the shoes of executed prisoners for the civilians in Germany. Therefore, we always listened in the morning for the call, "*Schuhe aus!*" ("Take off your shoes"), because that meant that a group of prisoners was about to be executed. When the call came, we then awaited the prayer after morning roll call so we could find out if any of our friends had been in the group liquidated in the early morning.

One day two Ukrainian prisoners were called to work in the kitchen to replace two other prisoners who had been transferred to a concentration camp. A little later two others were called to help divide the food among the prisoners. This gave us the chance to organize a means of communication between the rooms, because the prisoners who worked in the kitchen often met other prisoners, some who were about to be transferred to a concentration camp and others who came from Auschwitz to be interrogated. In this way much news was exchanged. Through the two who were helping divide the food, we had a chance to inform our friends in other cells about what was going on outside the prison.

Soon the winter came. It was very cold and humid, and the rooms were not heated. It was extremely dirty everywhere. There were lice and an epidemic broke out. Many prisoners died, and as a result, the transporting of prisoners to concentration camps stopped. All the Jewish prisoners were taken into the forest outside Krakow and there they were executed.

The big room used for collecting prisoners to be transported to Auschwitz was now empty, so the administration decided to put all Ukrainian prisoners there. So, after many months of being in several small rooms, we were all put into one extremely large room. Of course, we were all glad to be together, exchange information about our experiences, and discuss the situation.

When we entered the room we found many bowls in one corner. This was unusual because we had always been given bowls and spoons a few minutes before the food was distributed, and after we finished the food we returned them. It would be more convenient to have our own bowls, especially since we could then save part of the soup or coffee to have later. So we jumped on the bowls, hoping that we could use them all day. We were allowed to get water and clean the bowls, then we waited for the next distribution of soup. We still wondered why there were so many bowls in the room, and when the guard came to distribute the soup, we asked him.

He told us that these were not bowls for eating. Some of the Jewish prisoners had become ill from the epidemic and were too weak to use the buckets, so they were given bowls for urination which they emptied in the buckets. His explanation appalled us, and we threw our bowls away. Those who had already had soup served to them hurried to dump it into the bucket. One prisoner had just begun to eat, and he became the object of our jokes for some time. We told him that he was no longer an orthodox Christian and was not yet an orthodox Jew. He had eaten with a Christian spoon out of a Jewish bowl that had been used for urination. It was "gallows humor," but it helped us survive—we could still make jokes, however poor, in our horrible situation.

Our situation was truly like waiting for the gallows. As I have said before, the room we were now in had been used for gathering prisoners to be transported to Auschwitz. We feared that since the transporting of prisoners had been stopped only because of the epidemic, perhaps one morning we, too, would be ordered "Schuhe aus!" and be taken to the forest outside Krakow, what the Polish prisoners called na piachy, to be executed.

When we were transferred from the small cells into the large room, a group of Ukrainian prisoners was freed. Interrogation and investigation had been completed, and some prisoners who had pretended to have nothing to do with the Ukrainian underground movement were regarded by the Gestapo as having been victims of the general Gestapo action. They were freed. This gave us hope that there was a chance we, too, after a few more weeks or months, would be freed.

We were psychologically prepared for anything: to be freed and allowed to go home, to be freed and sent to work as slaves in German industry, to be executed, or to be transported to Auschwitz.

There was no reason to be constantly thinking about death, so we began to organize our daily lives to forget about our situation and what might await us.

As I have said, all we had to do was to clean our rooms and the bucket. We slept on pallets filled with straw, which was never changed. During the day they were all placed one on top of the other in a corner of the room. At night we put them out on the floor so that the whole floor was covered with pallets. In the morning, when the official gun for getting up sounded, everyone had to quickly put his pallet in the corner. Then the floor had to be mopped and the iron bucket had to be cleaned with sand and paper so that it looked like a mirror.

After this work had been completed, we had our coffee or tea for breakfast; the rest of the time we had for doing something else. The large group had divided into many smaller groups. Some of the groups sat and talked while others played cards or chess with sets made from pieces of paper. There were among us some writers and poets. They stayed near the window in the light and did their writing, but even the matter of writing paper was not simple. We received only one piece of toilet paper each. The writers used theirs for writing paper rather than for its natural use, and tried to encourage their friends to give them their toilet paper, too. The writers argued that this was a much more cultural use than that for which it had been intended.

One of our cellmates, Dr. Yaniv, today director of the Ukrainian Free University in Munich, wrote a collection of poems which he managed to send to his friends in the Ukrainian community. They were later published. Another friend, Daniel Tchaikovsky, had a collection of novels, and I myself had a collection of poems of satire and humor.

After lunch we would read whatever one had prepared for reading. Those who did not write were obliged to tell the rest stories, anecdotes, or jokes.

We seldom saw the prison guards, usually only during the morning and evening roll calls and when food was distributed, or when we had to fill and empty the buckets. Occasionally they would enter the cell to see if the floor and *kibel* ("bucket") were perfectly clean. Even then, they were arrogant and cruel. During roll call they checked the lines to see if they were perfectly straight. If one of the prisoners had his face a little too far to the front or back, a guard would kick him.

One guard, whom we called "Scheisse," was especially cruel. He was a half-idiot, and whatever was said to him, his answer was *"Scheisse."* That was the reason for his nickname.

The guards worked on three eight-hour shifts. For the first few weeks we were afraid to meet together, especially because of Herr Scheisse. However, one day when he looked through the "Judas" to see what we were doing in the cell, he caught one of our cellmates demonstrating his ability to stand on his head. Scheisse opened the door, came in, and looked at our friend. We were afraid that Scheisse would beat him, but he unexpectedly smiled and said, "I see that you know how to stand on your head, but you don't do it very well. I know how to do it, and I will show you how it should be done."

Herr Scheisse stood on his head, then asked us who had done it better. Of course, we applauded him and told him that he had done much better than our friend. We told him that we had expected him to do better since he was a German superman, the *uebermensch*, and that we knew whatever a German superman did would be done better than what an *untermensch* did.

As a result, Herr Scheisse became our friend and came into our cell every day for five or ten minutes. Our friend, whom Herr Scheisse called "Lux," would stand on his head, then Scheisse would do it. The result was always the same. We applauded Scheisse and declared that he was much better than Mr. Lux.

On Christmas Eve, 1942, thirty more Ukrainian prisoners were freed. Soon after, when we received the packages from the Ukrainian Red Cross and our secret mail, we got pieces of the Ukrainian newspaper, *Krakow Review*. In it we read that thirty prisoners of war of Ukrainian background had been released because they, former soldiers of the Red Army, had **volunteered to work in Germany. They had been sent to Ger-**

many to work in industry, the report said. Some of the names of these "prisoners of war" were even mentioned in the report, so we knew that they had really been freed. We had feared that they had been executed or sent to concentration camps, but now we knew that they had, instead, been sent to work as slaves in German industry.

The thirty released were soon replaced by thirty new Ukrainian prisoners brought from Lvov. From them we received information about the principle of "collective responsibility" as it had been applied by the Germans in Ukraine.

The incident which had brought this about was the attempted arrest of a leader in the Ukrainian underground. German police had entered his house and ordered him to surrender his guns. He dropped the two guns he had at his waist, and the Germans took him into custody.

Because the prison was not far from his house, they ordered him to walk with officers of the Gestapo in civilian clothes on either side of him, seeming to be his friends, and a uniformed SS man about five feet behind him. This way they felt no one would suspect that he was being taken to the prison.

When they got out onto the street, the Ukrainian drew a gun which he had kept hidden from the police under a rubber band on his shirt sleeve, and killed the two policemen walking beside him. He wounded the SS guard, but the guard also managed to wound him. He escaped, nevertheless, and the wounded SS guard died shortly thereafter.

Because of this incident, the Germans applied what they called "collective responsibility." Forty of the remaining Ukrainian prisoners in Lvov were selected, taken to a forest outside Lvov, and executed. The execution was brought to the attention of the people with the warning that collective responsibility would always be applied in cases of resistance to German authority, especially when one killed a German.

Five of the new Ukrainian prisoners, before they were transferred to Krakow, had been held in a prison in the second largest city of the western Ukraine, Ivano-Frankivske. There they had been interrogated personally by the chief of the Gestapo, Müller, who treated them extremely cruelly. They had been beaten and tortured. He told them that the

17

members of the Ukrainian underground movement, called by the Germans "Bandera-Bewegund" (an organization headed by Stepan Bandera), would be treated worse than the Jews because at least the Jews didn't resist German authority. The Jews died quietly, but the Ukrainians of the Bandera-Bewegund dared to resist the orders of the Führer.

Listening to all this news, we were beset at once by both hope and despair. On one hand, that a group had been released from the prison filled us with the hope that we, too, might one day be freed and taken to work in Germany. On the other hand, the threats by the chief of the Gestapo in Ivano-Frankivske that we would be mercilessly annihilated filled us with despair. However, we could do nothing but wait and see.

The winter was harsh and it was very cold in the cells, but nonetheless the prison was very seldom heated.

One day, while I was emptying the buckets, I saw a piece of a woolen blanket in the corridor. I asked the SS guard if I could take it to use for cleaning the floor. He told me I could, and after I got back into the cell, I extracted the threads from the blanket. With the threads, I started knitting some gloves. I had learned to knit in the Polish prison and now made use of the skill. Soon I had finished the gloves and had started a pullover.

One of the guards caught me knitting one day. He ordered me to show him what I was doing. I thought that I would be punished, but instead he asked me if I knew how to make all kinds of pullovers and gloves. I told him I did, and he ordered me to knit for him.

The next day he brought me a great deal of good wool yarn, locked me in his office, and left me there to make pullovers and gloves for his children. It was important to him because, during the war, there was a great shortage of knitted clothing.

This arrangement was to my advantage because his office was always heated. I had plenty of time to sit in the warm room and relax. Also, as payment for my work, he gave me an additional bowl of soup each day. This I divided with my cellmates. Each day three of them divided the extra bowl of soup.

We sat in groups of three. When one group was given the extra bowl of soup, the prisoner in the middle would give the man on his left twelve spoonfuls of soup and the man on his right the same. This was because we had found that there were just thirty-six spoonfuls of soup in a bowl.

Because of this extra bowl of soup, I learned how sensitive we had became to food. We received so little to eat that everyone was starving. Each spoonful of soup had special value.

One day the man in the middle of the group which had received the extra bowl of soup divided it out—twelve spoonfuls to the man on his left and twelve spoonfuls to the man on his right. After the division, he began to complain that there were only six spoonfuls left for him, that he was being cheated. We tried to convince him that he could be in the group receiving the extra bowl the next day and could be one of the men on the side, thus receiving his full twelve spoonfuls of soup. Nonetheless, he continued to complain bitterly that he was being cheated. This is hard for people living under normal conditions to understand. This abnormal psychological reaction, I noticed, was not limited just to food.

Once a week, as I have mentioned, we received a package from the Ukrainian Red Cross. In it were a little butter and cheese and about two pounds of bread. There were different ways of consuming it. Some ate everything in the package on Thursday—the day it was delivered. Others divided the food into enough portions for two or three days. Because I had always liked doing things systematically, I divided the bread into seven equal portions to be eaten one each morning with the cup of coffee we received for breakfast. One day one of the others said that I was a sadist because I ate when the others had nothing. It didn't help to explain that everyone had received the same amount that I had. From then on, I took my coffee into the corner of the room so no one could see that I was eating a piece of bread with my coffee. In the abnormal condition of starvation, the act of consuming twelve grams of bread by another makes even intelligent people irrational.

Time passed without any explanation of our situation. We continued to wonder what would happen to us.

In the spring we were ordered to begin work in a garden in a suburb of Krakow. We were taken there early in the morning in a police station wagon. Under the supervision of guards armed with machine guns we pulled all the weeds and made a garden where tomatoes were planted. The work was hard and the weather was hot.

One day we were ordered to plant an oak. It was early morning and the day was already extremely hot. I remarked to the German who was in the garden with us that it would do no good to plant the tree in such heat. He told me that he was a specialist and knew what he was doing; the oak *must* grow (*"muss wachsen!"*). Of course, the oak didn't obey him, but I knew better than to point that out to him.

The same thing happened to the tomatoes. A portion of the tomato plants came early one morning of another extremely hot day. I suggested that we plant them just before nightfall so that the plants could get used to the ground in the cool of the night and grow. Again he told me that he was a specialist and that I did not know what I was talking about. After about a week, half of the tomato plants had died and part of the garden was bare. I recalled what we had done when I had helped my parents with the gardening and I took branches from the plants that were growing and put them in the ground. The guard made fun of me; he told me that I was stupid and knew nothing about gardening. When my experiment was successful, he never mentioned it.

One day we had an opportunity to escape. While we were working, one shift of guards completed their time and left, but the next shift didn't come to replace them. When the day was over and it was time to go back to the prison, we realized that there were no guards. We were alone with only a fence around us.

When we started to discuss what we should do, we remembered the German policy of collective responsibility. We decided that it was probably no accident that the last shift guards had not come, that it was a Gestapo plan. Those who were caught trying to escape would be executed, and for everyone who did escape twelve or twenty others would be executed in his place. We decided not to try to escape.

We saw an SS guard passing the place and called him

and asked him to take us to the prison. He was startled because no one had ever asked him before to be taken to the prison. When we explained what had happened, he called the police administration and a truck came to take us back to the prison.

One of our friends found himself in a similar situation. He was taken every day by one of the guards to work in his apartment in town. He was accompanied by an armed guard both to and from the apartment. However, one day no guard came to take him back to the prison. The wife of the guard didn't know what to do, so he decided to walk. It was not far to the prison, and when he arrived, he knocked on the door and asked to be let in. Again, there was confusion, but when he explained, he was taken to his cell. Of course, he had come to the decision to return to the prison because of the collective responsibility. He would not take the opportunity of saving his own life by condemning his friends to death.

Chapter 2

AUSCHWITZ

The ten months of our imprisonment at Krakow came to an end.

On July 18, 1942, very early in the morning, a special SS guard came with a list. Twenty-four names were called. My name was among them. We were taken to the transport cell where we remained for two days.

On July 20 we were taken from the cell and loaded in a bus. A guard stood in the front of the bus facing us with his hands on his machine gun. Another guard stood in the back of the bus in the same position. Behind the bus was a car carrying two more SS guards armed with machine guns.

So we started out on our unknown journey. We were familiar with Krakow and could tell from the Wisla River and the Wawel Castle that we were traveling westward toward Germany.

Soon a violent thunderstorm broke. One of the prisoners fell against the side of the bus. The driver was alarmed by the noise and stopped the bus suddenly. The guards in the car, not knowing what was happening, started to shoot. The guards on the bus ordered us to fall to the floor with our hands up. Fortunately the shooting was only to raise an alarm and was not directed into the group of prisoners. We were searched and told to remain in the same position.

After about an hour of riding on the floor with our hands

up, the bus stopped and we were ordered out. The thunderstorm was over, and we were in front of a large camp surrounded by a wall and a double row of electrified barbed wire. Over the gate in front of us was a slogan in large letters which said *"Arbeit macht frei."* ("Work makes one free.") The implication was that if we worked we would be set free. However, we knew that what was said was not always what was meant in the case of the Nazis.

While we were wondering where we were, we noticed the inscription on the other side of the gate—"Auschwitz." It was then that we knew we had been transported to the concentration camp at Auschwitz, about thirty miles from Krakow in a place called Auschwitz by the Germans. In Polish the name of the place was Oswiencim.

The SS guard and members of the concentration camp administration were waiting for us. With them was a little man who, as we later found out, was a dwarf from a circus who had been brought to the camp for some reason. He was about three feet tall. He had a club and was running around and shouting. He ran over to us and began hitting one after another with his club.

The situation was not what it might seem on the surface. Because the dwarf was so small, any one of us could have killed him with a single kick, but we knew better than to do it. If we had, it would have been considered an act of resistance against the administration. The man who did it would be executed immediately. From the very beginning of our time at Auschwitz we learned to accept all manner of humiliation. In this case, the humiliation was because, although we were much stronger than the dwarf, we had to endure his beating us.

I suspect that this "demonstration" was arranged beforehand by the administration to give us a very clear and complete picture of our status at Auschwitz. It showed us that any member of the administration had complete power over the lives of prisoners and could do whatever he liked with them. We prisoners were not to resist in any way. We had to submit patiently or be killed.

We went through the camp gate, and the SS guard who had come with us gave the camp guard the list of our names.

We were counted, checked, and taken to a special block. We learned that each house was called a block.

There were three lines of blocks, eleven blocks in the first line, eleven in the second, and four on each end of the third row with a kitchen in the middle of the third row.

As we came into the reception room we were ordered to undress and go through a medical examination. Prisoners worked here. Usually members of the camp administration were German, but there were not enough to fill all the positions, so some Polish prisoners who claimed somehow to be of German descent were accepted as *Volksdeutsch*—German by national background. As such they were allowed to be members of the administration inside the camp.

When we arrived it was time for the morning roll call, so we were locked in the reception room until the roll call was finished. Through the windows we could see scores of prisoners placed in rows. They were all in dirty uniforms that looked like pajamas with black and white stripes. Their heads were totally shaven and they all looked like skeletons. At the ends of the lines of standing prisoners, there were some lying down. Some were still living; others were dead. The prisoners with administrative positions were running around kicking those prisoners in lines and shouting.

When the roll call was finished, we saw a big car come in front of the next building, the *krankenhaus* ("Hospital"), and the dead prisoners were brought up from the basement and loaded into the car. It was a quite large car and about one hundred bodies were thrown into it. Another car came and it, too, was loaded.

We asked the prisoner in charge of our group why it was so long before the dead prisoners were taken away, why they were kept so long in the basement. Because there were so many corpses, we assumed that it had been a long time since the cars had been to the hospital. He told us that three or four cars were loaded with corpses every day, and that we should not concern ourselves since we soon would be among the corpses.

Since roll call was finished, we began the reception procedure. The first step was the taking of a picture of each prisoner, but even this simple process was abused and made a special kind of torture for new prisoners. As each man got in the chair he was hit in the face instead of being told what position he should sit in. As he got up from the chair, he was hit in the face again and kicked from behind to keep him moving. This was our first lesson in the meaning of "concentration camp."

Next a *Volksdeutsch* took information from each prisoner to make a personnel card for him. When this *Volksdeutsch* asked for my address, I asked whether he wanted my family's address or my personal address since I no longer lived with my family. Laughing, he told me to give him the address to which I wanted my ashes sent since I would go to the crematorium in a few days.

Among the clerks we met some *Volksdeutsch* and some Polish prisoners who had lived in western Ukraine until it was occupied by Germany. They were very friendly and asked us questions about the war, where we were from, who we were, and so on. We expected to have them as friends since they had shared some of the same experiences we had. We especially expected the Polish prisoners to be friendly because of our help to them in Krakow. Some of the Ukrainian prisoners had been in the same cell with the leaders of the Polish underground in Montelupich Prison in Krakow and had let them use the secret mail we had organized to communicate with members of their Polish underground who had not yet been caught. This service was of great help to them. In one instance, a leader of the Polish underground movement had been caught and questioned by the Nazis. He, Colonel Sowa, was morally broken by the interrogation and every day gave names and addresses of more and more members of the Polish underground. Our secret mail let the other Polish leaders in Montelupich warn the members of the underground that it was very dangerous for them, and many of the Polish underground who would have otherwise been caught were thus saved. This was the reason that we expected the Polish prisoners to help us. We were the first group of Ukrainian prisoners to be brought to Auschwitz and we were informed that the Polish prisoners made up about 80 percent of the prison population.

Before the reception procedure started, we were ordered

to undress and put our clothes in a paper bag. Each bag was numbered and we received a piece of paper with the number on it. This was our prisoner number. We were lined up and told by a Gestapo man that all prisoners received a number and that we must remember that from this moment we had ceased to be human beings; we were only numbers and would be treated like numbers.

After completing the reception procedure, we were taken to a washroom and shaven from top to bottom. The shaving was very uncomfortable because the same razor was used to shave one or two hundred people. We were happy when it was all over.

Then we took a shower and received a uniform which was like pajamas and wooden shoes. There was also a cap made from the same material. We were each given two identical strips of material about one inch by 4 inches on which was a red triangle with the letter "P." We later found that this meant that we were Polish citizens. The "P" was followed by our prisoner number. My number was 49734. One of the two strips of material was to be placed on the upper left chest and the other on the right side of the pants at the level of the hand. This was so that from a distance one could see the number of the prisoner.

Chapter 3

BLOCK 11

So, dressed in the official uniform and instructed that we were no longer humans but only numbers to obey all orders without question, we were brought from the reception block to another block, Block 11. Block 11 was different from all the other blocks in that it was surrounded by an additional wall. It was at the end of the first row and, although it was in the camp, it had a separate gate.

We came through this gate into the front yard and were ordered into lines with Polish and Jewish prisoners transferred from other prisons. We were then taken to be placed in the block.

The clerk who had brought us to Block 11 had the personnel cards, and the clerks from Block 11 began to check the prisoners one by one. They spoke Polish, so we knew that the administration in this block were the *Volksdeutsch*, those who had, or pretended to have, a German background. One of them had a strip on his arm with the inscription *"blockältester."* This meant that he was the head of the prisoners of the block. The other was a *schreiber*, the secretary to the *blockältester*, who performed all the office procedures.

They called the first name on the list. It happened to be Bandera. This prisoner was the younger brother of the leader of our underground movement. His brother Stepan was much older than he and had become famous in 1934 when he was imprisoned and put on trial for the assassination of a member of the Polish government, Pieracki. The name Bandera was known to all Polish and Ukrainian people. When the secretary of the block saw his name, he ordered him to step to the front of the lines.

"You are a Bandera. You are the one who murdered our minister," the *schreiber* said, and hit the boy in the face. He fell to the ground. I was next to him and wanted to explain to the Polish *Volksdeutsch* that he was mistaken. This boy was Vasyl, not Stepan, and was now only nineteen years old and would have been a mere child in 1934. He could not have taken part in any assassination. I told him that this boy could not be responsible for what another Bandera had done. I also told him that we were all prisoners, and asked why should there by any discussion about what had happened so many years ago in Poland?

The clerk jumped me and hit me in the face. He told me that I should keep quiet or I would be next. He ordered the boy to go up on the porch of the block with him and stand at "attention" at the very end of the staircase. The clerk hit him again, and Vasyl fell to the concrete below. The secretary and two of his helpers then began to kick the bleeding body. It was all so unexpected.

There was a Polish prisoner who had been with us at Krakow, so we appealed to him. He said that he was afraid for his own life and didn't know what was going on anyway. We should decide among ourselves what to do.

Briefly and secretly we discussed the situation and decided that any attempt at defense would be useless. We had no legal protection and if we started to fight, we would be in an extremely dangerous position. There were only a few of us, and the block and camp were guarded by guards with machine guns. If we were not murdered by the members of the administration of the block, then we would all be shot before we could explain what was happening.

We were caught in a double ring of persecution. One ring was that of the Gestapo who, as we had heard from the chief of the Gestapo in Ivano-Frankivske, had decided that we members of the Ukrainian underground movement should be more mercilessly wiped out than the Jews because we had dared to resist Hitler's plans for the Ukraine. The second ring was that of the young Polish chauvinists, prisoners in a German concentration camp themselves, who had pretended to be of German descent. They took advantage of their position in the camp administration by persecuting the Ukrainian nationalists. From members of the Polish underground movement we had met in Montelupich Prison, we heard that the Polish organization worked in the concentration camp, so we still had hope that we would one day meet some of the members of the organization. We hoped that they would stop the wild, inhuman persecution of the Ukrainians by the Polish prisoners.

Soon we received the soup we were to have had for lunch. Everyone was extremely hungry since we had not eaten since early morning and it was now night. Nevertheless the soup was hard to eat. The only advantage was that the soup was like water and everyone was thirsty.

After we had finished the soup, the procedure of bringing prisoners into the building continued. We were called by our numbers one by one and told to go into the corridor to be assigned a place by the *blockälster* and his helpers.

As I watched the procedure before it was my turn, I noticed that as the prisoners entered the building they were asked by a tall prisoner if they were Ukrainian. We were arranged alphabetically so that the twenty-four of us were spread out among about a hundred other Polish, Jewish, French, and other prisoners. When a prisoner told this man that he was Ukrainian, the man kicked him in the face so that he fell into a room which I later found out was a bathroom. Inside the room were four other Polish prisoners waiting to beat and kick the Ukrainians. When it was my turn to enter the building, the tall prisoner asked me if I was a Ukrainian in Czech. I immediately realized that he was not Polish, but Czech, and answered him in Czech that I was from Prague. He was confused by my answer and asked me once more if I was Ukrainian even though I was from Prague. I told that I was from Prague, but that I was Ukrainian, but by that time I was already on the staircase, so he only kicked me from behind and I continued to run. I escaped the torture room.

When I came to the room I was to be in, I saw an awful

sight. The room was meant for about ten prisoners, but there were at least one hundred in it. There were bunk beds with three levels and instead of one prisoner on each level, there were four. Two prisoners lay with their heads at one end and two other prisoners lay with their heads at the other end. Thus there were twelve prisoners sleeping where there should have been three.

I was shown my place, and there were already three other prisoners on that bunk. I saw that not only was the linen extremely dirty, but also that there were thousands of lice.

In the same room were three or four other Ukrainian prisoners from my group. I was horrified at their appearance. They had fallen victim to the torturing in the bathroom which I had escaped. Their faces were covered with blood, their mouths and noses were broken—one had lost six teeth and another had many broken ribs. I realized how lucky I was that my psychological trick had helped me pass the Czech prisoner and escape this torture chamber. We all realized that we could expect nothing good to happen.

During the night we were awakened by an order that all Ukrainian prisoners were to go into the corridor. I realized that the purpose was to subject us to further beating by the Polish sadists and decided that if I had to die I would die here in the cell in the presence of other prisoners so that perhaps one of them might survive and report what was happening here. I changed my place and crawled under the bed. There I remained until morning when a cry "Up!" forced me to take my place in line for breakfast.

Immediately after breakfast we had to make our beds. The beds had to be made extremely well or the prisoners sleeping on that bed received five or ten lashes immediately or after night roll call.

When I got up I saw that only two of my bedmates were able to get up. The third was already dead. We found out that there was an epidemic of typhus and diarrhea and that many prisoners had died during the night.

The next morning we had roll call in the corridor of Block 11, then were divided into groups and transferred to other blocks. I was sent to Block 13A, and again went through the procedure for admitting prisoners to the block. Each prisoner was registered, his card was given to the *schreiber*, and he received a new strip with his prisoner number and triangle. The strips were already complete except for the letter which had to be placed on the triangle to designate the prisoner's nationality.

On the first day we had all received the letter "P" since we had all been brought from Krakow. Now we protested having the "P" since we were not Polish, but Ukrainian. If we had to die here, we wanted to die as Ukrainians, not as Poles. For our protest, we were all beaten and the clerk told us that if we were not Polish, then we were Russian. I told him that I was not Russian, that I had never lived in Russia, and that I had nothing to do with Russia. They asked me where I had been before I was arrested. I told them that I had been in Czechoslovakia, so they said I was Czech and gave me a "C."

So on our second day in the concentration camp our small group of twenty-four Ukrainian political prisoners had been divided into three groups according to the letter on the triangle. Some were "P" for Polish, some were "R" for Russian, and I was "C" for Czech.

After the registration procedure, all new prisoners were taken to the place where the roll calls were held. The roll call procedure was performed by prisoners who were members of the camp administration. Each of them was carrying something for beating—a club, a stick, a board. We were told to wait for the signal, then run as quickly as possible and take a place in a row. In a few minutes a column of ten straight lines, had to be formed. The prisoners of the administration ran along, kicking the prisoners to make them form their rows faster. After the lines were formed, they checked to see if the lines were really straight. If one's face was too far to the front, he was struck in the face with a club or stick. If he leaned a little too far back, he was kicked.

Then came the command, *"Muetzen ab!"* or *"Muetzen auf!"* This meant "Caps on!" or "Caps off!" Everyone had to take his cap off his head, lower his arm and hold his cap in his hand until the command, *"Muetzen auf!"* All this had to be done in exact unison. If one were a second or two late or early, he was kicked. After an hour of this kind of exercise, it was difficult to find a new prisoner whose face was not covered with blood.

After lunch the roll call procedure continued. This time one of my friends, Dr. Leonti Diakiv, a political prisoner, fainted and fell down. He had been a victim of the severe beatings of the night before. He had lost almost all his teeth, and had several broken ribs. Since he didn't regain consciousness he was put on a handcart and taken to the *krankenhaus*.

His story is very interesting. Nephew of a Ukrainian bishop, he had studied law and received his doctorate of law. He then decided to study theology and after receiving a doctorate of divinity, he decided to be a priest. It was 1940 and the western Ukraine was occupied by Russia. The NKVD was making massive arrests of Ukrainian students and Ukrainian intelligentsia suspected of being nationalists. A nationalist was defined by the NKVD as anyone who worked for the free Ukraine against Russian occupation. Dr. Diakiv, as a student of theology and a candidate for the priesthood, was regarded as an enemy of the proletariat, and was arrested with some other students.

After the long and cruel investigation, a public trial was held in Lvov. Some of the students brought to trial admitted being members of the Ukrainian underground movement.

During the trial the youngest of the defendants, Halyna Stolar, was permitted to express her opinion and the opinion of the other students. She admitted that she was a member of the Ukrainian underground movement and said that she and the other students were working for an independent Ukraine and a better way of life for the Ukrainian people; she did not, therefore, understand why they were being tried by Russians. She had been told that Russian Communists professed to be fighting for a better life for all working people. She said that since the Ukrainian upper class had been almost totally wiped out during the Polish and Russian occupations, almost all Ukrainians were working people. The landlords and rich people living in western Ukraine were Polish or Jewish. If the Russian Communists truly wanted to help the poor Ukrainian proletariat, they would arrest these representatives of the rich bourgeoisie, then go back to Moscow and let the Ukrainian proletariat organize a Ukrainian communist state.

The Russian judges and police took her statements as ridicule of their position, and she, and many others of the Ukrainian students on trial, were sentenced to death. The counsel for defense, following Russian trial procedure, appealed to the Supreme Council of the USSR for the sentence to be commuted.

Soon after this trial, Germany attacked Russia. In the first wave of the fighting, when the German army came to the outskirts of Lvov, the Russian secret police left the town in panic. When they found out that the German army had stopped outside the town for a time, they came back to the city and performed a macabre execution. All the prisoners were brought from the cells into the large prison yard and machine-gunned. The bloody bodies were put in the basement of the prison. Soon no one remained in the cells.

In the last group to be brought out into the prison yard was Dr. Diakiv, then about thirty years old. He and three girls and two other boys fell to the floor before they were hit by the machine gun bullets. They were covered by the bodies of the other prisoners as they fell. The NKVD prison guards locked the gate of the prison and left the town.

Soon the German army entered Lvov and the Ukrainian population broke down the gate of the prison. Inside they found a horrible sight—about five thousand bloody bodies stacked in the prison yard and basement. Only five prisoners had survived. Dr. Diakiv had survived the Russian persecution and imprisonment by a miracle.

When, on June 30, 1941, the establishment of the independent Ukraine was declared and a Ukrainian government was formed, Dr. Diakiv started to work in the Department of Education as head of the Department for Religious Affairs.

On September 15, 1941, during the massive arrests by the Gestapo, he was imprisoned once more, this time by Germans. He was taken to Krakow, and along with us was transferred to Auschwitz to be annihilated as an enemy of Nazi Germany. Here he had been barbarously beaten by the Polish chauvinists who pretended to be of German descent to gain a position in the camp administration. The Polish chauvinists regarded Ukrainians as enemies of their dream to build a

33

Polish empire from the Baltic to the Black Sea.

A few days after Dr. Diakiv was taken to the *krankenhaus* he was dead.

All prisoners had to work. There were many different kinds of work—cleaning streets, building new roads, constructing new buildings, working in industry, in the kitchen, cleaning offices, and so on. A group of prisoners at the same work was called a *kommando*. Some *kommandos* used the same prisoners all the time. The others, especially if the work was very hard, selected different prisoners for the *kommandos* each morning. Immediately after the morning roll call was finished, everyone was ordered to join his *kommando*. Those who belonged to the better *kommandos* ran as fast as they could to join them. Those who were left were put to the hard work. Most of the *kommandos* worked outside the main camp.

We were not sent to work the next day because we had to complete the procedure for transferring from Block 11 to our new blocks.

At 5:00 P.M. the *kommandos* working outside the main camp began pouring back in. There was a special ceremony for the return of the *kommandos*. Each *kommando* had to come through the main gate and march past the kitchen. In front of the kitchen was a symphony orchestra playing marches. It was thought that this was the best orchestra in the world at the time. Although this may seem like a joke, it is not unlikely that it was true.

When the decision was made to have an orchestra for propaganda purposes—such as when someone visited the camp—the best musicians among the prisoners were selected and added to the orchestra. In the camp were some of the best musicians from Vienna, Prague, Paris, Budapest, and all the capitals of Europe occupied by Germany. Hence, it is not at all unlikely that this was, indeed, the best orchestra in the world.

Each musician was vitally interested in retaining his skill and remaining in the orchestra. The members of the orchestra were given better food and were not sent to work—and thus escaped the kicking and beating—because they had to practice all day.

As I have said, the return of the prisoners from the work

was an especially macabre sight. On one side was an excellent orchestra playing beautiful marches and on the other side were the columns of prisoners. They marched in columns of five by five, each *kommando* separate so they could be checked by the SS man at the gate to make sure they had all returned. The first lines of the *kommandos* were made up of the strongest prisoners, the next were weaker—many forcing themselves not to fall down—and the last were prisoners carrying comrades who had died during the work. It was like a very large group of skeletons marching to the sound of beautiful music.

Members of the SS camp administration sat in front of the orchestra. To make a good impression, the *arbeitführers* forced all the prisoners to hold the marching rhythm. When a prisoner was unable to march as he should, he was kicked and beaten. Under the circumstances, the music seemed to ridicule the worth of human life, human relations, and the beauty of music itself.

In the period between 5:00 P.M., when the prisoners began returning from work, until the end of night roll call, the prisoners were not permitted to enter the blocks. They had to stay outside and wait for the roll call. When roll call was completed, they went into the rooms of the blocks in a very organized manner.

Those who had already entered the camp looked for a place and immediately lay down on the ground. It made no difference to them if it were dry or raining or snowing. Everyone was so exhausted that their only thought was to find a place to lie down and relax. Many died before time for roll call. No one cared.

Just as there were millions of lice in the beds, there were millions of fleas on the ground. As soon as a person lay down, he was immediately covered with fleas. Looking against the sun's rays, it seemed the whole area of sand was jumping up and down.

At 7:00 P.M. the night roll call started, and we saw again what we had seen the night before. All the prisoners were herded into ten lines, each block separated from the rest. The first part of the block was composed of those able to stand. In the middle were those only half alive, and at the end were the dead prisoners with their arms on their chests. The difference was that last night we had observed these procedures and now we were a part of them. We were no longer spectators, now we were beaten, kicked, forced to remain at attention, and not allowed to wipe blood off our faces—we were like all the rest.

The sleeping accommodations in each block were exactly the same. In our new block I had to sleep with three others on one bed again—two with their feet against my face and one on my side. The previous night I had been too tired to react to the crawling lice. Tonight I was a little more relaxed so when the lice attacked me, I began to kill them and keep a tally. After I got to one hundred, I was too exhausted to continue and fell asleep. When I awoke I saw that all my hunting had been in vain. There was no sign that I had killed any; there were still myriads of lice.

There was at that time an acute epidemic of diarrhea. The camp was closed; only entering transports were continued. There were no transfers of prisoners out. Hundreds and thousands of prisoners died from the epidemic.

The morning after my first night in the new block, I found that all three of my bunkmates were dead. When they didn't jump at the first whistle, I tried to awaken them, but in vain. I could not understand why, although this was the second night I had slept with them and used the same blankets. But I did not catch the epidemic; I somehow remained immune to the diarrhea.

None of my three bedmates was Ukrainian. Two were French and one was Jewish.

I found out that the other members of my group, Ukrainians, also did not catch the diarrhea for some reason. Again we applied gallows humor to make a joke. We decided that when the lice saw the letters "P," "R," or "C" on our uniforms, but heard that we were Ukrainian, they decided to wait until they were certain just what we were before they gave us diarrhea. Here I must add that we new prisoners had no underwear and had to sleep in our camp uniform with the identifying strips on them.

We soon became familiar with the structure of the camp administration. Since the Gestapo applied the principle of "self-rule," there was a double administration. The one was made up of the SS German police, and the other of the prisoners themselves. All prisoners were divided into blocks according to their house. As I mentioned, one building was called a block. All prisoners living in a house were administratively called as a unity a "block"—"Block 1," "Block 2," and so on. The buildings had two stories, so the prisoners were further divided into two groups in each block. For instance, the first floor would be called Block 5 and the upper floor would be Block 5A. There were always more prisoners on the upper floor because the upper floor had only two large rooms while the first floor had an office, bathrooms, and several small rooms. Usually there were about six hundred prisoners on the upper floor and only about four hundred on the first floor.

Each block had an average of one thousand prisoners. There were twenty-eight blocks, but Block 11 was used only for incoming prisoners. Three other blocks were used for the camp hospital, the kitchen, and the administration offices. Therefore only twenty-four blocks were actually occupied by regular prisoners.

The SS administration was headed by a *lagerführer*, the man responsible for the entire camp. Each block had an SS man attached to it called *blockführer*. The *blockführers* had only general control, so they usually came to inspect the block before and after the roll calls and occasionally during the day. The rest was in the hands of the prisoners' self rule.

At the head of the prisoners' self-rule administration was a *lagerälteste*. Each block had its *blockälteste*. The *blockälteste* had an assistant called a *schreiber*, a secretary who performed administrative office work in the block such as making notes on the cards when prisoners were transferred from one block to another, bringing the prisoners from one block to another, preparing the written reports for the roll calls, preparing an account of the prisoners in the block for food distribution, and so on.

Each block was divided into small groups called *stuben*. Each such group had a prisoner leader called a *stubendienst*.

Candidates for this self-rule administration were always selected from German prisoners. German prisoners, although they were prisoners like the others, were privileged in all respects. According to the German official policy, even the worst German criminal—a murderer—was better than the most intelligent non-German, be he a minister, secretary of state, or whatever. Therefore, even in a concentration camp, German prisoners were privileged. They were given positions in the self-rule administration and when the food was distributed they received a double portion of special food.

This was the structure for the general administration at the camp. The other structure was for the administration of the work. Each group of prisoners performing the same work was called, as I have mentioned, a *kommando* and had an SS man attached to it called a *kommandoführer*. In addition to the *kommandoführer*, each *kommando* had other foremen with different names according to grade. The smallest group had an overseer called a *forarbeiter*. Two or three of these small groups had a foreman called an *unterkapo*. The entire *kommando* was headed by a *kapo*. When it became necessary to join two or three *kommandos*, as when one *kommando* was constructing a building and another was making the material for the building, over all the *kapos* of the *kommandos* was an *oberkapo*. Each officer had a stripe around his left arm with the inscription of his rank.

In the beginning of the concentration camp, three hundred German prisoners had been brought in to fill all the administrative positions in the camp. It was soon realized, however, that it would be impossible to continue to fill the positions with Germans only. Therefore, the administration started using Polish prisoners who had declared that they were of German descent—the so-called *Volksdeutsch*. Also there were many prisoners who had lived in the part of Poland which had been cut off from Polish territory and incorporated into the German Reich. All people who lived in this part of Poland automatically became citizens of the German Reich and were called *Reichsdeutsch*. The positions not filled by natural-born Germans in the administration both inside and outside the camp were filled by these Polish *Volksdeutsch* and *Reichsdeutsch*.

I soon realized that the Germans liked the designation "*führer*." Of course, the first *Führer* was Adolf Hitler. Any member of the SS or Gestapo who had any position at all liked this title. Therefore, at the end of the war, whenever a man's name was found preceded by a title containing *führer—blockführer, arbeitführer, kommandoführer, appelführer*—it was immediately known that the man was an officer of the Gestapo. The title *führer* was never applied to a position held by a prisoner, even if he were German.

All positions in the administration held by prisoners were advantageous and lucrative. The officials were not obliged to work and were not persecuted by the SS or other prisoners. They had the opportunity to torture other prisoners. The *blockälteste* and the *stubendienst*—the prisoners working on the block—reported the number of prisoners in the block to the kitchen according to the morning roll call. They also distributed the food to the prisoners. There was always food left over in the evening because of prisoners who had died during the day. This remained for the disposal of the *blockälteste* and *stubendienst*. They could eat it themselves, distribute it to prisoners in special favor, or exchange it for something they needed like cigarettes or clothing.

At work, the other members of the administration I have mentioned—the *kapos, unterkapos,* and *forarbeiters*—were active. Although they were prisoners themselves, they were the wardens of the lives of every prisoner. It was a jungle and there was no protection. Whatever was done by a *kapo* or *unterkapo* was accepted by the SS without question.

No one was really interested in what was achieved by the prisoners' work. The basic reason for the work was to make the life of the prisoners as miserable as possible. This was achieved in part by keeping *"imnerlaufen,"* the so-called running tempo of the work. The prisoners always had to run—no matter what they were doing. The *kapos, unterkapos,* and *forarbeiters* walked around among the prisoners striking them with clubs and kicking them to remind them to keep up the "running tempo." If a prisoner was exhausted and fell, he was kicked until he stood up. Whenever it became evident that the prisoner was unable to stand up, one of the officers would hasten his death by putting a knee on his throat and pressing until the prisoner was unable to breathe. Very often there was simply an organized killing of prisoners because the extra food received by the *blockälteste* and *stubendienst* for the dead prisoner was shared with the *forarbeiter* who performed the killing. No one cared.

When a dead prisoner was found during roll call, all that was done was to check the number on his stripe, cross his number off the prison roll, and send his body to the crematorium. No one cared who had died—whether he was a criminal, a political prisoner, or a minister of a foreign country. And no one ever asked why this one had died.

When I returned to my room that night, a roommate who slept not far from my bed told me that he was a Polish political prisoner but that his father had been a commissioned officer in the Ukrainian army who, after World War I, had fled Ukraine during the Russian occupation. He came to Warsaw and enrolled in the Polish Army as a professional soldier. There he had married a Polish girl. My roommate, therefore, had been educated as a Polish boy and did not speak Ukrainian. Because of his father, though, he had a special sentiment for Ukrainians. Since he knew that I was Ukrainian, he came to talk to me and express his sympathy. During our conversation, he told me the story of a Polish prisoner in Block 11 who persecuted Ukrainians.

His first name was Kazik. He and his older brother were members of a well-situated Polish aristocratic family and had been students at the university in Warsaw. During the German occupation, because they were both active in Polish political life, they were imprisoned and brought to Auschwitz. As often happens, the younger brother was tall and strong and the older brother was even taller, but weaker.

When they were brought to Auschwitz, Kazik saw what was happening and heard about the advantages to those who pretended to be a *Volksdeutsch*. He quickly reported that he was of German descent, a *Volksdeutsch*, and was made a *forarbeiter*. His brother was in his *kommando*. The work was very hard, and after a few days, his brother could no longer run. Kazik, afraid that if he showed leniency toward his brother he would lose his position, forced his brother to keep running. When his brother was totally exhausted and fell down, unable to get up even though he was kicked, Kazik put his knee on his brother's throat and "helped" him die. The prisoners felt, even under these circumstances, that Kazik's actions were unusual and immoral. When the other Polish political prisoners expressed their condemnation of Kazik, he replied, "It is better to be a live pig than a dead hero."

Later, because Kazik had so graphically demonstrated his cruelty, he was transferred to Block 11 to be the secretary and to use his cruelty on the new prisoners.

My neighbor said that he would help me whenever he could, but that he was only a prisoner and so could not help much. His friendliness and sympathy had already helped me a great deal, both psychologically and morally.

He also explained to me why the triangles in front of the prisoners' numbers were different colors—some red, some black and some green. Red was given to political prisoners. Black was for those considered "asocial"—those who refused to work (like Gypsies) or who had escaped from the work and refused to follow the orders of the officers. Green was for criminals—murderers and others—who were serving their prison terms here in the concentration camp. Usually these were Germans, and although they were criminals, they were regarded here as the first class of prisoners and were made *blockälteste, kapo, unterkapo,* and so on. The violet triangles were for the religious enemies of national socialism. An especially large group wearing this color here, I later found out, were Jehovah's Witnesses. Rose red was for the sexual offenders, homosexuals and so on. Non-Jewish prisoners had a single triangle and Jewish prisoners had a double triangle formed like the star of David. On the triangle was the first letter of the nationality of each prisoner.

Chapter 4

AT WORK ON NEUBAU

Next morning, after the roll call, the Ukrainians who were scattered among several blocks were picked out by number and put into one group. This group was to work on Neubau. The fact that we were singled out and put in one group together let us know that once more we would be subject to special persecution. The whole *Neubaukommando* consisted of about one hundred prisoners.

We were taken through the gate and outside the camp. One of the prisoners close to me explained that nonetheless we were going to work in the main camp. The problem was that at that time the main camp was divided into two parts— one for the men and one for the women. The first row of blocks—1 through 10—was divided from the second and third rows by a wall with a separate gate; in order to get in this part one had to go out the main gate and come in the other gate at the far end. We were to work in this part of the camp on the construction project.

When the camp was started there were only the three buildings provided before the war for the Polish army. All the other buildings had been added. These first three buildings were only one-story houses and so they remained until the time I came to Auschwitz. Now these blocks had to be rebuilt, a second floor added, so they would look exactly like the twenty-five newer blocks.

When we left the main camp, I saw a group of prisoners surrounded by SS guards with machine guns and dogs. From the distance, I could hear their crying. When they came nearer I was confused because their voices sounded like those of children and even though they were grown, they looked like children. Their heads were all shaved and they were dressed in the work dress call *"kombinesons"* with the inscription "Soviet Union." Of course, I knew they could not have been soldiers of the Soviet Union.

The SS men were beating and kicking them and trying to keep them in lines. At the same time the dogs kept jumping on them and biting. They were all obviously terrified and were crying hysterically. Finally, when we passed this group, I saw that they were Jewish girls. Almost all of them were smeared with their own blood flowing from the wounds caused by the kicking and beating of the SS and the biting of the dogs. It was the first group of women prisoners I had seen, and I realized that the treatment of the women was exactly like that of the men. They were tortured and annihilated just like the men. The *arbeitsführer* was a commissioned officer—a German with a higher education.

Through the gate on the opposite side of the camp we came into the section where the women prisoners lived. When we were brought to the job during the day, the camp was almost totally empty. The work was continuing on the building of the second floors on Blocks 1 and 2. From my neighbor I found out that the *oberkapo* of the *kommando*, responsible for all work, was a Polish prisoner, Josef Kral, a professional builder who had pretended to be a *Volksdeutsch*. Also he had lived in the part annexed to the German Reich. Therefore, as a *Reichsdeutsch* by citizenship and a *Volksdeutsch* by national background, he had received this leading position. His helper for our group was *forarbeiter* Potkulsky, a young Polish student. He also had declared that he was of German descent, a *Volksdeutsch*.

We were divided into groups, each group was assigned a *forarbeiter*, and the groups were told what to do. Potkulsky's first question was, "Who is Bandera?" Bandera, the victim of the torturing of our first day in Block 11, reported and was again the target of torturing, this time by Potkulsky, Kral, and the other *forarbeiters* and *unterkapos*. He was first kicked and beaten, then put into a barrel of water. They took him out of the barrel of water and had him bring a bag of cement which they poured on him. Such brutality continued until, even though the work was not finished, he was half-dead. They did not kill him because they were afraid to arouse suspicion that it was done for revenge against the Ukrainians. They put him on a handcart and took him to the *krankenhaus*. He died before the next day.

The rest of us also became victims of persecution, but in a different way.

I was a member of the group assigned to take a truck outside and bring back the sand for the building. When our group of about twenty prisoners arrived at the place where the women prisoners were preparing the sand, the *forarbeiter* asked if anyone could speak German. I told him that I could, and he told me that he needed me because he wanted to talk to the *forarbeiter* of the female prisoners and she was German. He knew no German.

This was an exceptional opportunity for me because I had to remain near him at all times so I could translate what he said into German and what the female *forarbeiter* said into Polish.

Male prisoners were forbidden to talk to female prisoners even though they were close together in their work. This rule did not apply to the *forarbeiters* because they were privileged. The position of interpreter helped me very much on this first day of extremely hard work.

The next day a new Ukrainian prisoner was added to our group. He was the other brother of the Ukrainian leader Bandera. The two brothers had been arrested at the same time and had been with us in the prison at Krakow. When we were transferred to Auschwitz, only one was taken with us through some oversight. After two days the mistake was discovered and the other Bandera was transferred to Auschwitz also. He went through the receiving procedure and was added to our group.

When the *forarbeiters* and *unterkapos* found out that there was another Bandera, they repeated their treatment of his brother on him. Everything they had done to the younger

44

brother, they did also to this one. The *Forarbeiter* Potkulsky was especially cruel. After the man was already lying unconscious on the ground, Potkulsky jumped on his bloody body and said, "You are Bandera and I am *pantera.*" "*Pantera*" in Polish means "the panther." This man, Dr. Alex Bandera, was put on the handcart like his younger brother and taken to the hospital. He died the same night.

My accidental position as secret interpreter for *Forarbeiter* Kovalsky helped me a great deal. He didn't persecute me; on the other hand, he protected me because he was interested in keeping me close to him.

One day when we came to pick up the sand from the female prisoners I saw a girl with the letter "U" on her iniform. (It is interesting that the women were allowed to have the letter "U," but the male prisoners were not.) I asked her if she was Ukrainian. She told me she was and that she was horrified at all the cruelty here. I tried to console her and give her the hope that perhaps the girls would soon be freed. This had been the case in Lvov when we were first arrested. There were girls among us, but when we had been transferred to Auschwitz, all the girls had been freed. I hoped that she would soon be freed also. While I was talking to her I could not see that about two hundred feet behind us there was an SS guard looking around. He saw me talking to her and approached me. He shouted and got the attention of *Forarbeiter* Kovalsky. We both realized what was happening. The usual punishment for a prisoner talking to a girl was shooting. The SS guards liked to shoot a prisoner in front of the others to terrify them. So Kovalsky immediately hit me in the face and I fell to the ground; he pretended to begin kicking me. The SS guard saw this and was certain that *Forarbeiter* Kovalsky would execute me without his help, so he turned back. Kovalsky put me into the truck and warned me never to try to talk to a female prisoner again because had he not helped me I would have been killed by the SS man.

The next day, when I was working with the *Neubaukommando*, the other *forarbeiter* caught me and ordered me to work in bringing the cement to the machine in a running tempo. I had to run to the truck, lift a fifty-pound bag of cement, run with it to the machine, empty the bag, and run for another one. I did that for about an hour, but soon saw that this kind of work was beyond the capabilities of a prisoner—that in a couple of hours I would no longer be able to do anything. I knew that I would fall down and the *forarbeiter* would put his knee on my throat and kill me. I became hysterical and began to shout, "Come here and kill me now, you beast, you murderer! What are you waiting for? Don't wait until I fall down. Come kill me now as I am."

My shouting drew the attention of the other prisoners and, fortunately for me, the attention of *Forarbeiter* Kovalsky. He and the other *forarbeiter* came and asked me what was going on. I told them that it was impossible for a prisoner to do what had been demanded of me. It was perfectly clear that I would run back and forth like this for two or three hours, then I would be killed. They considered what I had said and, due to Kovalsky's intervention, I was replaced by three other prisoners and put back in Kovalsky's *kommando*.

The rest of the Ukrainian prisoners, however, continued to be subjected to unremitting persecution. Many were transferred to the *krankenhaus* where they died.

A few days before we had been transferred to Auschwitz, a large group of French prisoners, about twenty-five hundred, had been brought to the concentration camp from France. Among them were many of Polish descent, related to the old Polish émigrés. Although they were French citizens and participated in French social and political life, they spoke Polish as well as French. When they saw how brutally we were persecuted by other prisoners who shouted at us in Polish, they began to protest. They said that they had always thought that Poles were human, but now they could see that they were worse than beasts. Because of their protests, Kral, Potkulsky, and the others who were involved in the persecution decided to remove us from the presence of the other prisoners. On the order of *Oberkapo* Kral we were put into a special group and taken about three miles outside the main camp to a place called Babice.

Chapter 5

AT BABICE

The next morning we went to work in a place that used to be a Polish village called Babice. When the concentration camp had been built at Auschwitz, the village came under the administration of the camp officials. A farm was set up where the village had been; the farm was to supply the needs of the camp administration. Then, when I went to Babice, corn was being raised on the farm.

Our group was to build a new barn for storing the corn. Other groups were already at work. A group of female prisoners was harvesting the corn and another group of male prisoners was loading the prepared grain onto the carts. We were well aware that we had been sent here so that we might be annihilated far from most of the other prisoners.

Unexpectedly, when we arrived at Babice, the *forarbeiter* Michael came to me and said that he recognized me. He told me that he was a Ukrainian from Jaroslav and had met me there two years before. At that time I was lecturing to the Ukrainians living in Jaroslav. He told me that he had been a professional soldier in the Polish Army and that, as such, he was considered by the Gestapo to be a Polish patriot and was arrested and brought to Auschwitz. Here he had pretended to be Polish of German background and had been made a *forarbeiter*. He said that he would not persecute us and would try to help us if he could. He asked that I not tell the other prisoners what his real nationality was.

The *kapo* of our group was a real German, a murderer who had been sentenced to life imprisonment and then sent to the concentration camp. He was not interested in what was going on among the prisoners and left the persecution to the *forarbeiter*. He merely looked around for "organization." "Organization" was camp slang for stealing of food or some other article.

Because of our *forarbeiter*'s nationality and the disinterest of the *kapo*, we found that instead of the planned annihilation, we were able to relax in the relatively normal pattern of work in the concentration camp.

Our first task in building the new barn was to make the cement foundation for it.

We were brought to work, taken back to the main camp and guarded during the day by four SS men with dogs.

The place that we worked was in the form of a rectangle. At each corner of the rectangle one of the SS guards stood with his machine gun in his hand and his dog at his side. They had to make sure that no prisoner escaped.

There was no toilet and a prisoner who had need for one had to leave the imaginary rectangle. He had to report his intention to the guard, then was permitted to leave the rectangle for one minute. When the minute was up, the guard would begin to shoot at the prisoner if he were not back inside the rectangle. Therefore the prisoners always took care to count to about fifty, then jump quickly back inside the rectangle to avoid being hit by the bullets. Wanton killing of prisoners amused the SS guards.

Right next to us another *kommando* was working in a similar rectangle guarded by the SS men at each corner. There were many Jewish prisoners in this *kommando* and the guards took special pleasure in killing them. We later found out that if a prisoner tried to escape and was killed by an SS guard, the guard received one day off as a "reward." In order to get the day off, the guards in the *kommando* next to us would select one or two Jewish prisoners each day and order them to attempt to escape. When the prisoner was forced by kicking and beating to cross the imaginary line between the corners, the gurads started to shoot until he was killed. Because of this horrible practice, we had ample opportunity to see what sloppy marksmen the SS guards were.

One day an elderly Jewish prisoner was forced beyond the line, but he was too tired to run. He simply stopped where he was and put his hand into the air, waiting to be shot. After some shots were fired, he found that he had not been hit, so he started to run. However, he was too tired to go very far, so he stopped again. Again the guards shot at him and again they missed. This procedure of running and stopping and guards shooting went on at least ten more times. Each time the guards were unsuccessful in their attempts to kill the old man. Finally one of the SS men from our *kommando* put his gun on his knee and shot the man in the head.

That same cruel play was performed each day in the *kommando* next to us and also in another one in which many female prisoners were working. One or two prisoners would be forced into crossing the imaginary line and were shot so that the guards might receive their one or two days off.

When we began digging the holes for the cement for the foundation of the new barn, a friend of mine, Dr. Yatsiv, was working with me. He was a lawyer and had been a member of the Ukrainian government. He told me that he intended to go to the *krankenhaus* that night. I tried to persuade him not do it because we knew that when anyone went into the *krankenhaus*, it was very rare that he ever left alive. The physicians did not help the prisoners survive; they helped them die. He told me that it made no difference to him because he could not live very long anyway. He said that when we had first come into Auschwitz that the brutal beatings had cost him six teeth, several broken ribs, and damaged kidneys. He said that he was spitting up blood, so that even had he been released that day and put in a normal hospital he could not expect to survive for more than one or two months. He preferred to go to the *krankenhaus* and die as soon as possible.

When we returned to the main camp that night, he didn't even wait for the roll call, but immediately went and admitted himself voluntarily to the hospital. A few days later I found out that he had died.

Near where we were working was the house where a rich Polish landlord had lived. It was a big house with a garden surrounding it. It was now being used as a school for the police recruited from the Russian prisoners of war, the so-called Caucasian police. Since we needed a great deal of water for our work, we had to go to the well there. Each time a prisoner went for water he was accompanied by an SS guard. It happened that when a friend of mine went to fill the water barrels, he overheard the guard talking to the interpreter who worked in the school. They conversed in Ukrainian.

The interpreter was a Ukrainian and had been a soldier in the Russian army. He was fluent in German and since he was also fluent in Russian, the language familiar to Caucasians, Georgians, and Armenians, he was ordered to work here. On the return trip my friend asked the SS man if he were Ukrainian. The SS guard asked him why he wanted to know; what did he want from him? My friend told him that he wanted nothing but since he had overheard him talking to the interpreter in Ukrainian, he thought perhaps he would be interested in knowing that our group was made up of Ukrainian political prisoners and we were being annihilated by the persecution. My friend told the guard that he thought maybe he would help the Ukrainian prisoners. The SS man explained that he was Ukrainian from Bukovina. He said that when, in 1940, Bukovina was occupied by Russia, he had registered as a German in order to escape arrest by the NKVD. He, along with the other *Volksdeutsch,* real Germans, was transported to Germany in accordance with the terms of the agreement between Russia and Germany. This was how he happened to be a guard at Auschwitz. He asked my friend what he could do to help us. My friend told him that the only thing we wanted was for him to take a letter to the Ukrainian committee in Krakow secretly. After he had thought the situation over, he said that he would try, although it was an extremely dangerous thing to attempt. He told my friend to leave the letter in front of the gate to the house the next morning and he would try to deliver it for us.

That night we prepared a brief letter of information about where we were and what the conditions were. We listed the names of the members of our group who had already died.

The next day the guard picked up the letter. That night he covered forty kilometers on his bicycle and delivered the letter to the committee.

This was even more important to us than we had realized because of an event we had not known about. One of the Bandera brothers who had been so bestially murdered, Dr. Alex Bandera, had studied in Italy, had received his degree there, and had married an Italian girl. He had also become an Italian citizen. The girl he married was the niece of Minister Ciano.

When the committee received our description of how Dr. Bandera had died, they informed his wife. She called her uncle, Graf Ciano, who in turn called Himmler and asked him to explain how an Italian citizen, an Aryan, and a relative of the Italian Secretary of State, happened to be so brutally murdered in a German concentration camp.

Himmler ordered the Auschwitz administration to launch an investigation into what had happened. So, for the first, and probably only, time an investigation was undertaken to find out how a prisoner had died.

A few days later we were called to the political department for interrogation. We were all quite frightened since we did not know why we had been called; we knew that when a prisoner was taken to the political department he could expect to be tortured and then shot. When we were told that we were to be witnesses to what had happened to Dr. Alex Bandera, we relaxed a little. We described the incident, then *Oberkapo* Kral and *Forarbeiter* Potkulsky were brought for interrogation.

Since *Oberkapo* Kral was both a *Volksdeutsch* and a *Reichsdeutsch* (German by descent and citizenship), he was beaten only slightly during the interrogation, and then transferred to Block 11 for the duration of the investigation. It was found that *Forarbeiter* Potkulsky was not of German descent, that he had pretended to be a *Volksdeutsch*, and that he had used his position for torturing Dr. Bandera. The Gestapo applied their usual methods of interrogation to him.

I was waiting in the next room to be interrogated after Potkulsky, and saw him when they took him to the washroom. He was covered with blood and fainting. It was the only time in my life that I saw a victim of horrible torturing and was unable to feel any pity.

I said, "Now, Potkulsky, do you know what it feels like to be so tortured?"

"I am dying," was his only answer.

"Bandera was dying, too, when you jumped on him and kicked him," I said. "He was nearer to death than you are now, yet you had no pity on him."

To this I got no answer. Potkulsky died in the washroom.

We later found out that Dr. Bandera's wife had received a report from the Germans through the Italian government that her husband had been arrested in the Ukraine as the brother of Stepan Bandera, the leader of the Ukrainian underground movement. It was not known, they reported, that he was an Italian citizen. When he had been transferred from the prison in Lvov to Auschwitz he had been placed in a special section for prisoners who were only to work under good conditions and not to be persecuted, so they said. Unfortunately, there was a severe epidemic of diarrhea, the report continued, and he had fallen victim to it and had died shortly thereafter. Thus the investigation was closed.

This unusual investigation concerning the murder of a prisoner helped relieve some of the pressure on the Ukrainian prisoners. The news of Potkulsky's death spread quickly among the Polish members of the administration and made them afraid to continue the kind of treatment they had given Vasyl and Alex Bandera, lest they end up as did Potkulsky.

The new attitude among the Polish members of the administration was of special benefit to a second group of Ukrainian prisoners, about twenty-five, who were transferred from Krakow to Auschwitz three weeks later. They also were put in Block 11, but they were not subjected to the special hunting of Ukrainians. Everyone was beaten so that they would "learn where they had been put and what they must expect," but the Ukrainians were not singled out for any special torturing this time.

The first group of Ukrainian prisoners had received numbers beginning with 49,000. My number was 49,734. The second group received numbers beginning with 57,000. During the roll call we learned that the number of prisoners in the main camp remained the same—about 20,000—during the previous three weeks. Since, as I have mentioned, the camp was closed because of the epidemic, this meant that about 8,000 prisoners had died during this time and an equal number had been transported in to replace them.

During the work at Babice, I witnessed an unusual incident of solidarity between a German prisoner and another prisoner. The group of women prisoners came near where we ate our lunch to get their food because it was more convenient for the SS men to distribute all the food in one location. Food had been provided that day for about fifty women prisoners who had come to work in the morning, but during the work a number of them had died. The SS guard discovered this, and decided to take one barrel of the soup away. The *kapo*, a German prisoner herself, protested vehemently. She told the guard that so many had died that it was proof that the work was extremely hard and therefore the extra food should be distributed among those who had managed to survive. Many of them would die the next day. The guard pushed her away, but she began to shout at him and told him that her brother had been killed fighting bravely in the German army against Russia. She said that the SS man was a coward who would not fight in the army where he should be, but could only demonstrate his "bravery" here by fighting women and helpless prisoners. The SS was confused by her attack and gave her the soup. She distributed it among the prisoners. We were near enough that we could see and hear all that was happening, and we were amazed to the point of disbelief. In our part of the camp we almost never encountered sympathy from the German prisoners toward the non-German prisoners.

During the Bandera investigation we twenty (five were already dead) Ukrainian prisoners had been held in the camp, and had been replaced in the work at Babice by other prisoners. When the investigation was completed we returned to the Neubau inside the main camp.

The special persecution of the Ukrainians had stopped, so now we were free to find ways of surviving each succeeding day in spite of the extremely hard work.

At the work on the Neubau I once had a chance to observe a special characteristic of human nature. The work assigned to us was the building of the second floors on Blocks 1 and 2. At that time there was a wooden barracks between these two blocks in which on one side was the laundry and on the other side the showers for the new female prisoners. Here the women were brought, undressed, and shaved. When it was necessary for us to take material from one block to another, the easiest way was to walk across the roof of this wooden barrack. During the trips across the roof, the prisoners made an opening to see what was happening inside. We were all young boys, and although we were extremely tired from the weeks of hard work and terrified by the thought of further beating and dying, almost all of us still wanted our chance to kneel on the roof and watch the *kapos* and "barbers" shave the naked women. The "barbers" were German criminals, but even the *blockaltester* liked to come into the barracks and have a good time at the expense of the horrified naked girls. One day one of the French prisoners lay down by the opening to watch and stayed too long. The *kapo* noticed that something was wrong and came up on the roof to check. He found the Frenchman lying there and kicked him so that he fell down on the cement to his death. Even that incident didn't discourage us from looking.

One day we saw a macabre scene. A group of very young women had been brought in and among them were four beautiful and seemingly aristocratic girls. When they were ordered to undress and submit to the shaving by the "barbers" and *kapos*, they became so hysterical that they jumped out of the room and ran between the barracks and the next block. They were followed by the *kapos* and SS guards with their dogs and, of course, in just a few minutes returned bloodied from being kicked and beaten by the guards and bitten by the dogs.

The second group of Ukrainian prisoners who had come about three weeks after the first group was luckier than the first because, as a result of Potkulsky's death during the interrogation and the shaving and imprisonment of *oberkapo* Kral in the basement of Block 11 (*Reichsdeutsch* were permitted to wear their hair long), Kazik and the others were afraid to do any more to the Ukrainians than they did to all the other prisoners.

About the time the second group of Ukrainians and a large group of Polish prisoners came to Auschwitz, two prisoners who had worked in the *Politische Abteilung* died as a result of the epidemic. At the same time a prisoner who had worked in the kitchen died, too. The SS guard who came with the workers from the *Politische Abteilung* was in great need of helpers and, since all other prisoners were already working, he simply asked the new prisoners if any of them were fluent in German. Two of the Ukrainians, M. Klymyshyn and Z. Vynnycky, immediately reported that they were, and after a special accelerated registration procedure, they were put to work in the *Politische Abteilung*.

The *Politische Abteilung* was an office of the Gestapo in the concentration camp. Usually a prisoner was sent to Auschwitz to stay until he died. An investigation into his case would have been performed before he was sent to Auschwitz, and then the matter was closed. However, sometimes something new would be discovered, and then the *Politische Abteilung* would be responsible for interrogations about the matter. They were also responsible for the political conduct of the prisoners and prepared the list of prisoners who, for one reason or another, were to be executed. Therefore everyone, including the German prisoners, feared the *Politische Abteilung* because everyone knew that extremely barbaric methods of interrogation were employed there. When a prisoner was brought there, his greeting was being hit with rubber clubs by two strong SS guards until he fell to the floor unconscious. He was revived by having water thrown on him and then asked his name and personal information. Depending on the case, different methods were used after that. Very often the infamous Boger machine was used. It was named after a member of the *Politische Abteilung* who told the prisoners that he had a talking machine that would make them speak. The machine was a big wheel like those used in medieval times. The victim was strapped to it, turned upside down, and tortured. After several hours of this, he was usually removed from the wheel and carried out on a stretcher.

Prisoners were employed as clerks in the *Politische Abteilung*. The clerks were usually German, but some were Polish, and Boger's secretary was a Jewish girl, Maryla Rosenthal. She was to have been married to a non-Jewish German, but was arrested a few days before the wedding and brought to the concentration camp. The clerks had nothing to do with the torturing and interrogation, but the mere fact that they worked in the *Politische Abteilung* made them feared by all other prisoners. Their positions gave them access to all kinds of information about the structure of the concentration camp as well as various other kinds of information. So, when the two Ukrainians were unexpectedly employed there, it was of great advantage to the others, because everyone was afraid to persecute anyone who had a friend in the *Politische Abteilung*.

Another member of the second group of Ukrainians was hired to work in the kitchen. This also helped us. He helped us "organize" a means of stealing food from the kitchen and the kitchen storage.

At the end of August, 1942 the construction of the second floors for the first two blocks was completed. At that time some administrative changes were made. Up to then the women had been housed in this walled portion of the camp in Blocks 1 through 10. When the second floors were finished, the women were moved to another part of the camp called Birkenau, and the wall was torn down. Men prisoners were placed in the blocks the women had occupied and thus there were then only men in the main camp.

The transfer of the women from the first ten blocks gave the camp officials a chance to disinfect the main camp. The first ten blocks were disinfected with chemicals, then the men from the second row of blocks were showered, smeared with disinfectants, and given clean clothes. They were then put in the first row of blocks. This procedure was followed row by row until the whole camp had been disinfected. At the same time the prisoners were carefully checked, and those who were suspected of being sick were sent to the *krankenhaus* to die. Anyway, the disinfection improved the camp greatly because it eliminated the epidemic and the billions of fleas and lice ceased to exist.

In the disinfection of the camp, the tendency of the Germans toward precision was especially beneficial. When the first group of men went to be disinfected, they were taken completely naked and were not allowed to take anything with them, not even a piece of paper. They remained for three days and had the chemicals applied over their whole bodies three times each day. Even the food was delivered only to the gate by the prisoners from the kitchen. There it was sprayed with chemicals by a special commission of doctors. After about thirty minutes, the naked prisoners were allowed to come out and get the food. All this careful precision totally wiped out the epidemic.

After about a month at Auschwitz, with help from our friends in the kitchen and the *Politische Abteilung*, and from working in different *kommandos*, we had a very good idea about the administration of the concentration camp at Auschwitz.

Chapter 6

STRUCTURE OF THE CAMP AT AUSCHWITZ AND LIVING CONDITIONS

The concentration camp at Auschwitz (Oswiencim in Polish) was founded in 1940 on marshland between the Wisla River and its tributary, the small River Sola. It was close to the boundary between Germany and Poland and during the fighting at the beginning of September, 1939 the town had been destroyed.

At the outskirts of the town there were barracks for the detachment of the Polish army. These three barracks were taken by the Gestapo and made the nucleus of the new concentration camp. A rectangle of about three hundred meters by five hundred meters was surrounded by a wall about ten meters (thirty feet) high. This was the main camp, which was called by the official code KL Au 1.

Inside the concrete wall were two other fences of barbed wire, also about ten meters high. The first one was about ten feet from the wall and the second was about ten feet from the first. They were electrically charged and well lighted at night. In front of the first row of barbed wire was a strip of gravel with a warning posted on it that it was not to be crossed. Only those who wished to commit suicide by running into the electrically charged fence or being shot by a guard risked crossing the gravel strip.

Twelve towers were spaced along the cement wall, one on each corner and two on each side. Each was equipped with searchlights and was always occupied by an SS guard armed with a machine gun. If a prisoner happened to make it to the fence without being killed by the electrical charge, a guard showered him with bullets to make sure that he was killed before he got over the fence.

When the first group of prisoners came to Auschwitz from the concentration camp at Dachau, which had been in existence for a long time, twenty-five more houses were built and the first three were expanded to include second floors so that all twenty-eight looked exactly alike.

The beds in each block were bunks with three tiers with four prisoners sleeping in each bunk, two in each direction. This meant that in the space where there would normally have been one bed for one prisoner, twelve prisoners slept.

The main camp had a capacity of twenty to twenty-five thousand prisoners. It soon became evident that this was not enough. The administration of the camp took over an adjoining eight thousand acres and a second section was built onto the camp. It was given the official code KL Au 2. Although it was just another part of Auschwitz, it was known by the name Birkenau or, in Polish, Brzezinki.

The generally accepted abbreviation for concentration camp was KZ, but the officially used abbreviation was KL. This was to purposely mislead people into thinking that the concentration camps were simply camps for people working in German under war conditions.

In front of the camp there ran a railroad which went from Krakow to Germany and Prague, Czechoslovakia. Between the railroad and the camp there was a magnificent palace built for the *kommandant* of the camp. It effectively hid the camp. Only those who were aware of the situation knew that behind the beautiful villa was not the industry that people were led to believe was there, but the concentration camp Auschwitz, the horrible "Mill of Death."

Outside the camp there were wooden barracks which housed the offices of the Gestapo and the *Politische Abteilung*. Also outside the camp, but on one of the corners of the rectangle, was a big crematorium.

Birkenau, the other part of Auschwitz, officially coded KL

Au 2, was built in 1941-42 about three miles from the main camp. It had a completely different function, and consequently a completely different arrangement. A large area was surrounded by barbed wire and divided into two parts by a railroad. In the middle there was a railroad station. This was a dead end railroad, a branch off the regular tracks. On one side of the railroad in one small part of the camp there were buildings for housing non-Jewish prisoners, similar to the buildings in the main camp. The other, larger, part of the camp was covered with many larger buildings, many of which had been stables used by the Polish army before the war. The same type of beds was used here so that there were three tiers of bunks with four prisoners sleeping in each bunk.

Birkenau was divided into several sections. One section was occupied by Gypsies. Gypsies, according to the Nazis, were a race which had to be annihilated because they were asocial. However, since many of them were German citizens, they were not executed immediately but were brought to Birkenau and told they would work in German industry. The other section of the camp was occupied by Jewish families brought from Teresienstadt in Czechoslovakia. During the early days of the camp, even the Jewish population was divided into different ranks. The highly privileged group of Jewish prisoners were those who were German citizens. A second privileged group was made up of Jews from Czechoslovakia. The lowest group of Jews was made up of those brought from eastern European countries, especially Poland.

All non-Jewish prisoners, called officially Aryan, were brought to the main camp to live or die under concentration camp conditions. It was quite different for the Jewish prisoners. They were brought into Birkenau by train—five to ten thousand every day. Once they arrived they were divided into two main groups—women with children, and men. The *kommandant* was usually present and selected from those who arrived each day about fifty (not more than one hundred) to be sent to the main camp as regular prisoners. All the rest were ordered into the big area of Birkenau and told to undress so they might undergo the process of disinfection—to take a shower and change clothes. They were then taken by groups into a big room which looked exactly like a shower room, but when the room was filled with prisoners the doors were closed and the gas Cyclon B was released through holes in the floor and ceiling. In about ten minutes all who were in the room would be dead. A special *kommando* called the *sonder-kommando*, consisting of about eight hundred strong young Jewish prisoners selected from the Jewish transports, transfer-red the corpses from the gas chambers to the crematoria.

In Birkenau there were four large crematoria, always in operation, but since they were not capable of cremating all the corpses, two piles were built on the ends of the camp. A pile was built by placing a layer of corpses, then a layer of wood, then another layer of corpses, then another layer of wood, and so on until the pile was about two stories high. It was then thoroughly doused with kerosene and lit. By the time the second pile was completed, the first would be finished burning. The members of the *sonderkommando* would clean up the few remaining bones and start a new pile. In this way, during the existence of Birkenau (from 1942 until January, 1945), about three million Jewish people died. The children under twelve were not gassed, but were taken to the cre-matoria immediately. There they were undressed and pushed into the fire. After a few minutes of the extremely high heat, there would remain only an ash where there had been a child.

Jewish prisoners destined for the gas chambers were not registered individually. A general report was kept in the office of the Gestapo which read that on such-and-such a date five or ten thousand prisoners from a given place were transferred to the concentration camp. Only the Jews sent to the main camp received an individual number preceded by a Star of David.

The *sonderkommando* which transferred the bodies from the gas chambers to the crematoria and the two piles was re-cruited from among the Jewish boys. The strongest from each transport were selected for this *kommando* and they were given good food and drink. However, they only worked for about three or four months. After this time they were all liquidated and replaced by another group. This precaution was taken to insure that no one from the *sonderkommando* would escape and report what was happening at Birkenau to those outside.

All Jewish prisoners were ordered to write letters to their

families in Germany, in the territories occupied by Germany, and even to relatives in America before they were put through the "disinfection process." In these letters they were to tell their relatives that they were living in good circumstances, that they had to work, but the work was not hard, and they were paid for it, that they were allowed to live together as a family in their own room, that they received good food, and that there was a theater they were allowed to attend on weekends. The prisoners were told to date the letters months in advance. For instance, if a prisoner were brought in during January, 1943, his letter would be dated March or April, 1943, long after he would have been gassed. The letters were collected by the Gestapo and mailed through the International Red Cross on the dates they had been dated. It left the impression that all these people were still alive, living in relatively good condition in a camp for workers.

All the clothing and other belongings of the gassed Jewish prisoners were gathered into one spot, called "Canada" by the prisoners. The "Canada"— *kommando*, after the articles were disinfected, sorted everything and then it was distributed by the German Red Cross to the civilian German population. For the prisoners, the "Canada" was the most important source of "organization." The term "organizing" was slang among the prisoners for stealing. Hence, when a prisoner stole some bread he had "organized" some bread. The prisoners who worked on the sorting of all these articles in "Canada" often would steal something, smuggle it into the main camp, exchange it for bread or sausage from one working in industry, and be pleased with his success. The one who then had the "organized" article would in turn sell it to the civilians for whiskey. The *blockältester* and other members of the camp administration would give bread and soup for the whiskey.

Often the "Canada" contained some really precious items. Most of the Jewish men were businessmen, and when they were arrested and transferred to Birkenau, they would try to take as many of their personal belongings with them as they could. Most of the jewelry was taken by the ranking SS men. Many would come secretly and steal things for themselves before the others came.

The story was told that a rich Jewish gentleman from

Amsterdam brought a diamond necklace worth at least $100,000 into Birkenau. He had tried to hide it on his body, but it was found when he was ordered to undress. Since it was worth so much, the prisoners working on the "Canada," and even the SS men, were afraid to try to smuggle it out of the camp, so they reported it and gave it to the *kommandant* of the camp. He made a gift of the necklace to Marshal Goering's daughter. Of course, Goering, his wife, and daughter all knew where such a precious gift came from. For this same purpose the chief of the Gestapo, Himmler, came from time to time to "see" Auschwitz.

When Birkenau was first opened, there was a special Russian section. Here were kept the Russian political commissars, called in Russian *"politruks."* They were transferred here to the conditions of the concentration camp after they were discovered among the Russian prisoners of war. They were in the hands of the German political leaders and therefore were submitted to an especially harsh regime. In the spring of 1943 this part of the camp ceased to exist after the last prisoner died from the cold.

Many of the Russian prisoners had been born in Siberia and had grown up under extremely harsh natural conditions, but even they were not able to survive. This was because in addition to working at the running tempo all day, after the night roll call they were submitted to one or two hours of exercises in which they crawled on their knees and elbows in the snow. After these exercises, they were all thoroughly wet and exhausted. Then they had to stand for one or two hours at attention in the cold which often was at the hard frost level. They were not permitted to wear shoes during the winter, so there they stood in the extreme cold, soaking wet, barefooted, and with shaven heads.

THE WORKING DAY

The prisoners were awakened at 4:00 A.M. by a whistle. Everyone immediately jumped from bed at the sound of the whistle to escape being aroused by a rubber club. Beds were made and coffee was consumed.

The prisoners were then marched out in front of the

block to prepare for roll call. This preparation took about an hour and was performed by the *blockältester* and other members of the administration. As I have mentioned, this preparation took the form of hitting, beating, and kicking the prisoners.

Next the prisoners were taken to the central location for roll call where the procedure of preparation was continued in the presence of the SS men who helped the administration do again what they had done an hour before.

Roll call officially started at 7:00 A.M. The prisoners had to take their positions by block in front of the kitchen in ten straight lines. The *blockältester* reported the number of prisoners to the *blockführer*. He checked the numbers, then reported to a *reportführer* and the *reportführer* reported to the *kommandant* of the camp.

In the morning after the *reportführer* had reported to the *kommandant*, the roll call was usually over. At night roll call the situation was different because, from time to time, they would be unable to find one or more prisoners. This was especially important because most of the prisoners worked outside the main body of the camp, and they felt it necessary to find out exactly where a prisoner was so that there would be no discrepancy between the roll on the paper and the number of prisoners counted. Until the difference was reconciled, all prisoners had to remain. When it was suspected that a prisoner had tried to escape an alarm was sounded, and the SS guards were sent out to check the area surrounding the camp. For that reason the night roll call was often quite long.

In the spring of 1942, one of the night roll calls lasted thirty-six hours. About five hundred of the prisoners were unable to stand that long and fell down and died. The cause of the lengthy roll call was an escape attempt by one of the prisoners. He had tried to follow the underground tunnels to the river. He had hoped that when he reached the river he would be able to come out and escape. He found out that at the end of the tunnel was a covering of iron bars. Knowing what awaited him if he returned to the camp, he decided to die there at the end of the tunnel. It took the police dogs thirty-six hours to find his body.

On the second or third day after I came to Auschwitz, the

night roll call lasted three hours. No one explained why, but the next night after the report had been made to the *kommandant*, we were ordered to remain.

Two guards and an interpreter came with a prisoner, and the interpreter explained, first in German then in Polish, that the prisoner was a Czech about fifty years old and had tried to escape while he was working on the camp's farm. As soon as it was discovered that he had disappeared, his wife, mother, and daughter who lived in Czechoslovakia not far from the camp were arrested and brought here. He was soon found and brought back, too. After the explanation, the prisoner was kicked and beaten in front of each block, then was taken to a gallows which had been built before. The interpreter explained that since he had tried to escape, his mother, wife, and daughter would be hanged in Birkenau in front of the women prisoners at the same time he was being hanged here. After he had been hanged, the prisoners were forced to march in front of the gallows and take a look at him so they would remember what happened to a prisoner who tried to escape.

Roll call was held every morning and every evening regardless of the weather. Even in the winter we had to stand bareheaded whether it was raining or snowing.

The quality of the food we were given was measured by the Nazis in calories. According to the witnesses who testified against the Nazis after the war, the average diet at Auschwitz was eight hundred calories. The body of a worker usually requires about three thousand calories. This meant that the prisoners who worked much harder than ordinary laborers and were submitted to persecution during the work and the roll calls, received less than one-third the required food.

Food was distributed three times a day, and twice a week the prisoners received *zulage*, one additional portion. In the morning we received a cup of coffee. Between noon and 1:00 P.M. we received one quarter of a gallon of soup. After the evening roll call we received a cup of tea, twenty-five decagrams of bread, and three decagrams of margarine. In addition to that regular nightly meal, twice a week we received about twenty-five additional decagrams of bread and ten decagrams of sausage. The "coffee" was made from acorns, the "bread" was made from a mixture of corn and rye flour and wild chestnuts and sawdust, and the "tea" was made from tree leaves. The sausages and the meat in the soup was horse meat. At the beginning of the war the Russian army had used horses. When they were confronted with tanks, many of the horses were killed. The corpses were loaded onto a train and brought to the concentration camps for making sausage and soup for the prisoners.

Prisoners who had money on deposit were permitted to buy ten cigarettes each week. It was a comfort to the smokers, but it especially helped the non-smokers, for we could exchange our cigarettes for bread and soup. Prisoners who worked in the camp administration were especially good prospects, because they wanted the cigarettes and had the extra soup left because of the prisoners who had died during the day. For my ten cigarettes I could buy three pieces of bread and one portion of soup. The generally accepted rate of exchange was one portion of soup for one cigarette, and one portion of bread for three cigarettes.

One who ate only the portion provided for him would soon fall victim to starvation. The only hope was to find friends who could help him or "organize" himself, that is, steal some additional portion of bread or soup from the kitchen, from the storehouses, or from another place. The average prisoner was not able to take the chances necessary to get the extra portions. Therefore the camp was divided into two extremely unequal groups. In one group were the average prisoners who, after a few days or weeks in the camp looked like skeletons. They were called in the camp jargon *"musulmen."* These prisoners looked like living skeletons who were already in another world just waiting for the time when their bodies would fall down and die. In the other, much smaller, group were the prisoners known as "prominents." These were either members of the administration or those in good *kommandos* who were able to "organize" additional food each day.

Some of the prisoners tried to divide the bread we received after night roll call into two parts—one part to be eaten at night and the other to be eaten in the morning when we received only coffee. The second portion the prisoner would often hide under his pillow. It was usually stolen during the night. When a prisoner was caught stealing from another prisoner, he was placed on the floor and immediately given twenty-five lashes. After a second or third offense he was beaten to death. This was a law of self-protection among the prisoners. It was felt that each prisoner was entitled to at least the basic food provided him.

Similar punishment was meted out by the SS guards when a prisoner was caught stealing from the storehouses or the kitchen. If one was caught stealing, after the night roll call he would be stretched out over a chair and held by two prisoners from the administration and given twenty-five lashes with rubber clubs wielded by two SS men. For the average prisoner, surviving this punishment was not difficult. What was difficult was jumping out of bed the next morning when the whistle sounded. This resulted in further kicking and beating by the *stubendienst* and *blockältester*. If the prisoner survived this, then he would perhaps be unable to perform as required at the roll call and would be beaten again. If he made it that far, he usually died or was helped to die sometime during the roll call or the work later. Some prisoners survived thie punishment with the help of friends who either did their work for them, or paid the *blockältester* to let them stay in the block under the pretense of going to the *krankenhaus* or to the *Politische Abteilung* for interrogation.

We quickly found that in order to survive it was necessary to have connections in the administration and resources to pay for favors to save not only one's own life, but also the lives of one's friends as well. All of us in both Ukrainian groups had been members of the underground movement and had worked together before the war and were used to thinking of each other's welfare. That is the basic reason we were better able to survive than any of the other prisoners.

One block was occupied by the *krankenhaus*, the camp hospital. There were many good physicians working there, and it was said no hospital in Europe had more specialists than this one. This was because, at that time, most of the doctors in Europe were Jewish. When they were arrested they were not sent to the gas chambers, but were sent to the *krankenhaus* as specialists. Male prisoners, either medical students or young physicians, worked as nurses. They had all the necessary equipment and supplies, but the problem was that no one was interested in helping the prisoners. Only those with friends who could pay the doctors or nurses with bread, margarine, or something else could hope to survive a stay in the *krankenhaus*. Usually prisoners who reported to the hospital were registered and, then sometime within the next twenty-four hours, received a poisonous injection.

Twice a week there was an inspection of the prisoners in the hospital by a German doctor. All prisoners were ordered to stand in the corridor for roll call where the German doctor inspected them. When, in the doctor's opinion, a prisoner was dangerously ill and endangering others in the hospital, he was ordered to undress and get into a truck waiting outside the door. He was delivered to the gas chamber at Birkenau. The prisoners who could not stand up for the roll call were given injections before the inspection, and as soon as they died were taken to the basement to be delivered to the crematorium.

The official punishment (given by the SS guards) consisted of lashes with rubber clubs, time in the *strafkommando*, and finally execution. For a minor infraction such as stealing bread from the kitchen, not following the prescribed form for roll call, not coming to attention when a guard passed, etc., the prisoner was punished after the night roll call with twenty-five lashes. Sometimes, while waiting for his lashes, the prisoner had to stand with his hands bound to the gallows. The harshest punishment, other than execution, was being sent to work in the *strafkommando*. This was a *kommando* made up of prisoners who were being punished. They were given the especially harsh work in Birkenau to do. Very few survived the work. Execution was performed in two ways—hanging and shooting.

Hanging was performed on groups of prisoners, always less than twelve at one time. Hanging was done after night roll call in the presence of all the prisoners who had to stand at attention and watch the hanging, then march in front of the gallows and view the prisoners hanged. When there was a group larger than twelve to be executed, they were sent to Block 11 where they were shot. A specialist in this form of execution was SS officer Palitsch. The type of gun used was the kind ordinarily used in the butchery of cattle—spring action with a needle in the end. Prisoners to be executed in this way were placed in the basement of Block 11 naked and fed nothing for three days. The basement was filled with prisoners so that it was impossible to walk. The treatment was designed to break any spirit of resistance the prisoners might have. At the end of the three days, the prisoners were taken, one at a time, into the courtyard and ordered to kneel. The SS executioner placed the gun of the back of the prisoner's head and shot the needle into his brain. The next prisoner was brought, ordered to push aside the body of the previous prisoner, kneel, and then was executed in the same way. All the bodies were loaded onto a truck and taken to the crematorium. When we reported for roll call we would try to guess how many had been executed from the blood on the road in front of Block 11.

The main camp had only one crematorium. When there were too many bodies to be taken care of at the main camp, they were loaded onto a truck and taken to Birkenau where there were four crematoria and two piles.

The prisoners were executed not only for what they themselves did, as in the case of those who tried somehow to escape from the camp, but sometimes were victims of the "collective responsibility."

One time there was a *kommando* of land engineering specialists, made up of twelve men, making maps of the area round the camp. They worked individually, each with his own SS guard. One of the guards liked to drink, and asked the prisoner he was guarding if he could "organize" whiskey for him. The prisoner got the whiskey, and after a few days of providing whiskey for the guard, the prisoner added poison to it and the guard died. The prisoner dressed in the dead guard's clothes and managed to escape from the area before he was discovered. In the ensuing investigation it was found that when the prisoner had been initially arrested, he had given a false name and address so that now the "collective responsibility" could not be applied to his family or to anyone close to him politically or nationally. So another form of responsibility took effect. All the other land engineers, although they had not known the escaped prisoner personally and had not worked near him or been a part of his escape, were ordered to go on the left wing after roll call. They were marched to Block 11 and hanged the next morning.

Among the SS guards there were different kinds of people. There were those who enjoyed persecuting the prisoners—some were even wholeheartedly sadistic—and there were a few one met from time to time who were friendly and, although they obeyed orders, tried not to be especially hard on the prisoners.

The two most feared guards were Kaduk and Palitsch. Kaduk was a simple SS man who was feared by the average prisoners, the *musulmen*. Until his trial in 1957, I, along with a number of other prisoners, thought that his name—Kaduk—was a nickname, for it means "devil" in the Silesian dialect. During the trial we found out that Kaduk was his real name. It is very appropriate, in my opinion, for it accurately describes his nature. Every day he would come to the camp and look for an excuse to persecute a prisoner—he was not doing his work, he was not dressed properly, he did not greet him respectfully—and when he found such an excuse he would beat the prisoner with his rubber club and kick him until he fell to the ground. When the prisoner had fallen, Kaduk was satisfied.

Palitsch was a different sort of man. He was an SS commissioned officer and was feared by the prominent prisoners. He was the one who performed the executions with the needle gun on Block 11. He came to Block 11 every morning to perform these executions. They gave him a great deal of pleasure. He walked around the camp each day and looked for prominent prisoners he thought should be executed. He wrote down their prisoner numbers on a piece of paper without alerting them in any way. Whenever there were not enough prisoners to be executed because of their own misdeeds, Palitsch turned in his list. The prisoners on it, who had no reason to suspect that they would be called, were told to go to the left wing and were, the next day, executed by Palitsch with his needle gun. So whenever a prominent prisoner saw Palitsch he would try to get away in order that he would not be seen by this horrible sadist and be added to his list.

Chapter 7

NEW KOMMANDOS

At the end of my first month at Auschwitz, the work on Blocks 1, 2 and 3 had been completed. At that time the prisoners in the *Neubaukommando* were divided among other *kommandoes*. I was sent to a *kommando* called "*strassenreinigers*." This means "street cleaners." Our job was to clean the streets inside the camp and also the streets between the buildings outside the camp, in the area where the SS guards lived. The work was not as hard as that on the Neubau, and an experienced prisoner soon could see that because the *strassenreinigers* were so spread out the *kapo* could not always see each prisoner. All that the prisoner had to do was to watch carefully, and if he saw an SS guard or a *kapo* coming, he could pretend to work very diligently. The prisoners had to be especially careful of the SS guards. When one approached within about ten feet, the prisoner had to stand at attention, remove his cap, and remain in that position until the guard passed. If the guard stopped, the prisoner had to report his number and the work that he was doing. Otherwise, we fared much better than we had before.

One time, while I was cleaning the yard in front of the SS kitchen, I noticed the smell of sausage. The smell was bad and I found in the garbage can a piece of sausage which had been there at least two or three days. It was the rainy season, so in addition to the sausage and some potatoes, there was water in the garbage can. After some deliberation, I decided that roses were for smelling and sausage was for eating, so I disregarded the bad smell and ate the sausage and potatoes and drank the rainwater. Unfortunately, it was too much for my shrunken stomach and I vomited. I went on a diet the next day and ate nothing, so I felt much better in just one day. In addition, I saved my portion of bread and gave my portion of soup to a friend. He tried to persuade me to continue my diet through the next day so that he could again have my portion of soup, but I decided that I was well enough to eat my own soup.

When I had been transferred to the new *kommando*, I also had been transferred to a new block. Here I was lucky. When my *blockschreiber* took me with my personal card to the *schreiber* of the new block, he told him a joke. While the new *schreiber* was still laughing heartily, I told him a joke also. He liked it and said that I should come to him each night after roll call and tell him more jokes. So each night I told him a juicy Russian or Polish joke, and he paid me for the entertainment with an extra portion of soup. He also agreed to take care of my portion of bread overnight so I could eat it with my coffee in the morning. This was a big help to me. Even though I have since written a number of books and articles and have received my honorarium since that time, I have never been so rewarded as I was for my juicy jokes in a German concentration camp.

Chapter 8

BEKLEIDUNGSWERKSTÄTTE

Compared to other *kommandos*, cleaning the streets in and around the camp was not so hard or bad. However, fall was coming to an end and the weather was getting worse. Very often there was rain and we had to continue working in it, so often the street cleaners came back to the camp wet and had to remain wet for at least an hour during the night roll call. Often the temperatures were so low that this was almost playing with our lives. Therefore I began to look around for another *kommando* to work in.

Two of my friends had found among the prisoners a Ukrainian who had been a member of the Polish army. When he came to the concentration camp he had preferred to pretend that he was Polish. He was a good shoemaker by profession, and was sent to work in a special place called the *bekleidungswerkstatte*. This was a clothing workshop. Outside the main camp was a large building where all kinds of artisans were sent to work—tailors, shoemakers, ropemakers, and others. The work was good because one had only to fill his quota of suits or shoes or whatever for the day. If he did that he was not particularly persecuted. Only when he was unable to finish his work was he punished at the end of the day with five, ten, or fifteen lashes with a rubber club. The most important advantage of this work was that it was inside, and the prisoners did not suffer from the effects of the weather.

Our friend, Shevchuk, the one responsible for the shoe repairs, agreed to take two from our group, a lawyer and a bookkeeper, who had reported that they were shoemakers even though they had no idea how to make or repair shoes. He took care of them by assigning them only the simplest repairs and helping them with their work. At the end of the day he would report that they had done what was assigned to them. After a few weeks of his help, they became semi-proficient, and he was able to pretend that they were indeed shoemakers.

When I heard about them, I decided that that was where I would like to work. I told the boss of the clothing workshop that I was a professional tailor and would like to work there. In the morning several of us went to the workshop and were lined up. There were at least fifteen candidates to be tailors. When the kapo began asking each prisoner how long he had been a tailor, I saw that the other prisoners were real tailors from Paris, Brussels, Rome, and other big cities with at least ten or fifteen years of experience. I had only three years of experience to report. The kapo selected ten of them and sent the rest of us to different work.

I was ordered to go into the backyard where there was a new wooden barracks which had been recently completed. There were many boards lying around which were no longer needed. A group of about ten prisoners, myself among them, had to store these boards in a big room. During the work I talked to the other young prisoners and found out that they were Jewish students from Belgium. Before they had been sent here, they had received letters from relatives in Auschwitz. The letters had said that it was a work camp, and this had given the students the hope that they could survive long enough for the International Jewish Organization to exchange German prisoners taken in Africa by the Americans and British for them. After a few days in Auschwitz, the students saw how things really were.

The few days we spent storing the boards were comparatively tolerable. When we finished, we were ordered to clean the big yard, and it was during that time that I witnessed a horrible game played by two German sadists. The kapo of the bekleidungswerkstätte was a master civilian who had been a prisoner himself in Auschwitz, but had been freed and had remained to work in Auschwitz as a civilian. After the work in the workshop had begun, he and another member of the administration would complete the inspection, then come out into the courtyard with a big German police dog.

First they looked around among the prisoners, then they selected their first victim from among the Jewish prisoners. They ordered him to run, then sent the dog after him. The dog would catch him and tear at his legs, arms, and rest of his body until he fell in his own blood. The two men would kick him until he stood up and began to run again. This would continue until the prisoner was no longer able to stand. Then they did a victory dance on his dead body and the corpse would be taken away.

Both these Germans were political prisoners. The *bekleidungswerkstätte kapo* was a German communist with a university education. In their sadistic game they were aided by the *forarbeiter* of the work in the backyard, a Polish *Volksdeutsch*.

One day I found myself in the same situation that St. Peter had found himself when Jesus was brought to the court and Peter was asked if he were a member of Jesus's group. The Polish *forarbeiter* called to me and asked if it were true that I was a Ukrainian member of the Bandera group. This question posed a problem for me. My pride told me to say, "Yes, I am," and face the consequences. On the other hand, I knew that he was a simple criminal, that no one would see how I died here, and that it was useless to try to keep one's pride before such a man. On the contrary, it would be better to think about saving life. I asked him why he had asked such a question as if he were a member of the *Politische Abteilung*. He said that if I were a Ukrainian, he wanted me to take part in the game with the dog instead of a Jew. I told him that I was from Lvov where, as he knew, many Polish people lived. He could see that I was more fluent in Polish than he, so how could he suspect that I was not Polish? He agreed and did not make me a part of his game. I tried to keep far away from him from then on.

In another part of the backyard, the prisoners were sorting shoes. Shoes left by the Jewish prisoners gassed at Birkenau were loaded onto a truck and brought here. The prisoners had to separate the pile of shoes into left and right shoes and place them in rows. The area was covered with thousands of shoes. The prisoners had to run to one side, remember three shoes, then run back and try to find their mates. When the pairs were matched, they were bound together and put on a truck to be delivered somewhere in the town for distribution to the German civilian population. When the mates were not found, the odd shoes were delivered to the shoemakers as material for repairs.

Of course it was very difficult to match the shoes because the prisoners were under such psychological pressure that they spent more time looking for the guards to avoid being beaten than they did looking at the shoes. Perhaps a quarter of the shoes were matched and delivered. The other three-quarters were used for repairing other shoes.

I worked there for a few days and the one day the *kapo* of the *bekleidungswerkstätte* asked if there were someone among the prisoners who could make pullovers. I immediately reported and he took me inside the workshop and placed me between the tailors and the ropemakers. I had to pretend to be a ropemaker during the inspection, but since I was under his protection nothing could happen to me. Soon he brought me some wool, and I began a pullover for him. It took me many days to finish it because he changed his mind so often. He would find better material, take that which I had completed and give it to someone or sell it, and have me start again with the new material. I was glad for the opportunity because the *forarbeiters*, when they saw that I was working for this horrible sadist, preferred to leave me alone. When he was not with me, I used the wool he did not like to make pullovers for myself to sell to the other prisoners for bread. It was another source of extra food.

When I was transferred to Block 22 I met another sadist. He was the *blockältester*, a German communist political prisoner who had a university education. The Polish prisoners called him "one who kicks and bites," because he liked to hit the prisoners in the face so hard that they would fall, then use the opportunity to kick them with his boots. Once when we were having the inspection of our clothing, a French prisoner fell victim to his cruelty. We had had to prepare a new stripe with our prisoner number on it. The French prisoner didn't speak German and couldn't get a new one in time, so he decided to fix his old one with a pen. It was raining and the ink ran and made his stripe look very bad. When the *blockältester* came to him and saw his prisoner number looking so bad, he hit the Frenchman in the face so hard that he fell down. Then the *blockältester* began to kick him. The Frenchman kept crying in French, "Comrade, comrade!" He was probably also a Communist political prisoner, just as the *blockältester*, but even this kinship didn't help him. The German had no sympathy for the Frenchman, although both probably belonged to the same political movement, and both were victims of the same political ideology, Nazism.

Chapter 9

DMYTRO

Among the groups of prisoners sent to Auschwitz, there was one group that was different from all the others. Most prisoners were sent to the concentration camps for an indefinite period, usually until they died. However, this other group of prisoners, called "cocks," were to be held in the concentration camps for only three months. These were prisoners from eastern Europe, especially the Ukraine, who had been sent to work as slaves in Germany and had tried to escape. They were recaptured, then sent to Auschwitz for three months. If they survived, they were taken back to the same or similar work in Germany. Because of their relatively short stay, they were called "cocks"—they seemed like cocks that jumped on a gate, then ran away.

At least 80 percent of them were from western Ukraine. It was quite easy to recognize them because they had a different listing and had no triangle on the stripes before their numbers. They were housed in a wooden barracks between blocks.

From 1942 until 1943, they were housed in the main camp, and in late 1943 they were transferred to Birkenau.

The period between the end of the night roll call and the distribution of food and the gong for sleep was the time allowed for visiting. Most, especially the *musulmen*, preferred to lie down or at least sit somewhere to relieve their exhaustion.

Those who were still able to walk liked to look around to see if they might find some of their friends and listen to the news. After surviving my time as *musulman*, I did the same.

One evening while I was walking around, I met my cousin Dmytro. I saw from the number on his chest that he was not a political prisoner, but a "cock." He told me that he had been captured in the western Ukraine and had been sent to Germany to work. He had tried to escape, but was recaptured and transferred to Auschwitz.

After a few weeks, we met another of our friends, Roman Klachkivsky. Roman was a leader in the underground movement in Volhynia, the northwestern part of Ukraine.

The first time I had met Roman, before World War II, I had been struck by his resemblance to Dmytro. He was a physical double for him. When, during that time, Roman had found it necessary to escape the Polish police, Dmytro had given him some of his clothing and his personal documents. We put him in the forest near the border where Dmytro was working at that time, and it was very simple for Roman to cross into Czechoslovakia. When the war began, Roman came back to Volhynia and continued his work in the underground movement.

Roman told us that the underground movement was growing in its work against Germany and, as one of its leaders, he had been caught and transferred to Auschwitz. I noticed that Dmytro was listening very carefully to everything Roman was saying. Roman pointed out that there were thousands of members prepared to fight to the death against the Nazis, but that there was an acute need for good leaders.

The next evening, after the roll call, Dmytro came to me and told me that he had something important to discuss with Roman and me. We found Roman and went to a section of the camp where the French prisoners usually rested. This was for our own protection, because almost all the French prisoners suffered from diarrhea and were unable to attend to their hygiene. The horrible odor that surrounded them made it unlikely that any other prisoners would visit their section. None of the French prisoners understood Ukrainian, so we found a place among them and began to talk.

Dmytro said that he had been thinking about what Roman had told us all day. He said that we were all in the same situation and faced the same dangers, except that Roman and I would be there indefinitely, and he would be sent back to Germany in three months. After his return to the work in Germany, he thought that it would be not so difficult to attempt another escape, perhaps a successful one this time, and go back to Ukraine and join the underground movement. Roman had said, however, that the need was for leaders and he was only a simple member. He told us that he had decided, therefore, that he and Roman must change clothes and he would become Roman the political prisoner and Roman would become Dmytro the "cock." He would stay here, and Roman would thus have the chance to go back to Ukraine.

Roman was shocked, and he told Dmytro that he would not buy his freedom with the life of another. He said he would pay for his actions himself with death if necessary. Dmytro countered Roman's protests with simple logic. He said that he was not exchanging himself for a man, but that he was sacrificing his freedom for a leader who could help the underground movement more than he could. This he felt was what was important—that the underground movement be helped in the best way possible. Eventually Roman agreed to go along with the plan.

For the next three days they exchanged personal information in case one or the other was questioned. After they completed this exchange, they then secretly exchanged clothes. Thus Roman became Dmytro and Dmytro became Roman. During our activities of the next few days we found out, with a great deal of relief, that no one suspected what had been done or even thought that it was possible.

Then something happened that we had not taken into account in our plans—the left wing.

One evening after roll call Roman's number appeared on the special list and he was told to go on the left wing. Dmytro, pretending to be Roman, obeyed the order and was taken to Block 11. Immediately after roll call Roman came to me. He was very agitated and told me that he was going to the *kommandant* and explain what had been done so that Dmytro's execution would be prevented. I told him that that course of action would be useless for all concerned because the only result of his explanation would be that he and Dmytro both would be executed. Our only course of action was to wait and see what would happen. The only question now was whether Dmytro was strong enough to stand up under the interrogation, or whether he would break under the torture he would receive in preparation for the execution.

The next evening after roll call the prisoners were not dismissed but were ordered to remain for the execution. We saw Dmytro led to the gallows by the SS guards. His face, chest, and pants were smeared with blood. He had been brutally tortured before the execution to prevent him from shouting anti-German slogans. He walked as if he were going home. He knew where Roman and I stood during roll call, and glanced at us and smiled. When he had been placed on the chair with the rope around his neck, he glanced at us and smiled one more. It seemed to me, at that time, that he was Jesus Christ looking down from the cross.

Two weeks later the "cock" Dmytro was freed and transferred to a labor camp in Germany. About a month later, I received a brief greeting from Dmytro in Volhynia.

One year later a new group of prisoners brought to Auschwitz reported that the underground movement in Volhynia had become involved in open guerilla warfare against the Germans at the end of 1942. At that time the UPA, the Ukrainian Insurgent Army, had been born.

This movement was to deal many heavy blows to the Nazis. In May, 1943, Victor Lutze, Hitler's SA chief, was killed by the UPA when he came to Volhynia to plan anti-partisan action.

On March 12, 1945, Colonel Klym Savur, the commander-in-chief of the UPA in Volhynia, fell in battle against the Russian NKVD. It was revealed in an official communiqué issued by the UPA that the real name of Colonel Klym Savur was Dmytro Klachkivsky. The members of the underground movement who had known Klachkivsky since his childhood were puzzled. They had always known him as Roman Klachkivsky, and did not understand why he had started using Dmytro as his first name when he had escaped from the German work camp.

There were other cases of prisoners exchanging uniforms

and numbers, but I never heard of another case in which a man died for his friend. This method was often used by Polish prisoners who had friends in the *Politische Abteilung* who would let them know when a "cock" had died during the day. The Polish prisoner informed would exchange uniforms with the corpse. The Polish prisoner's number, now on the corpse, would be crossed off as dead during the night roll call, and the Polish prisoner would have only a few weeks' wait for his release as a "cock." This was an extremely risky thing to do, as those who were caught at it were executed immediately.

In order to prevent further exchanges, in 1943 the administration decided to tattoo the number on the left forearm of each prisoner. All prisoners except the *Reichsdeutsch* and the Germans received a tattoo on the left forearm. The prisoners who did the tattooing were careless unless they were paid with a portion of bread. Jewish prisoners had a triangle placed in front of their numbers; non-Jewish prisoners received the number only. The "cocks" received no tattoo and continued to wear the number without a triangle on their clothes.

After the work, when the dead prisoners were placed at the end of the columns for night roll call, their left forearms had to be placed on their chests so that the SS guard checking the numbers of the dead prisoners could easily match the number on the list with the number on the body.

The numbers were given to the prisoners consecutively and, therefore, played an important psychological role. The numbers soon passed 100,000 and those prisoners whose numbers were over 100,000 were called "millionaires" by the others. These newest prisoners were the targets for all kinds of abuse. The prisoners with the low number, those who had been here the longest, were respected not only by the new prisoners but also by the *kapos*. When a *kapo* saw a low number on a prisoner, he would assume that there must have been a reason that the prisoner had survived so long and would be unwilling to come into conflict with him.

Our friends who were clerks in the *Politische Abteilung* told us that there were several lists of prisoners, each beginning with "1." We were on one list, female prisoners were on another, "cocks" on another. Jewish family prisoners brought from Theresienstadt in Czechoslovakia were on a separate list, and the gypsies were on a separate list, too. As I have mentioned, the Jewish prisoners brought for immediate liquidation by gassing were not listed by individual numbers. The practice of giving these victims a stripe with a prisoner number on it was only a psychological trick. When they undressed and put their clothes in a paper bag they received two copies of the prisoner's individual number; one had to be put on the paper bag with the clothes and the other was held in the hand to present after returning from the bathroom. This was done in order to make the prisoners believe that they really were going to the showers instead of a gas chamber. These numbers remained unused for a while, then they were given to a new group of victims. Instead of individually listing these victims, they were mentioned in a special group of reports which read, "On (date) at (place) 5,000 or 10,000 prisoners were transferred to KL Au 1."

The small group of Jewish prisoners actually sent to the concentration camp at the beginning received consecutive numbers mixed among the numbers of the non-Jewish Aryan prisoners. Later they were listed separately on a list with numbers preceded by the letter A. When this list reached 20,000, a second list was started with numbers preceded by the letter B. Again it was applied only to those who were actually sent to the camp, and not to those who were sent to the gas chamber.

Chapter 10

ONE SUNDAY'S WORK

Usually, Sundays were free from the regular work. On this day the prisoners cleaned their clothes and shoes and took care of replacing the stripes with the prisoner numbers. Also, once a month the prisoners were allowed to write a brief, eleven-line letter to their families. The letters always had to begin with, "I am well and everything is fine." This simple work took almost all day because the clothes had to be repaired and the prisoners had to wait in line to use the needle to do their repairing. Also it was necessary to stand in line a long time before shaving. There were only a few barbers to shave the prisoners; the procedure was very unpleasant because one blade was used for shaving at least one hundred prisoners and each of those one hundred prisoners had to be shaved from top to bottom. Also, the beds and rooms had to be cleaned before the roll call which was usually a little early on Sundays. One group of prisoners was organized for special work on Sunday. Usually prisoners being punished were sent, but if there were not enough of them, the *kapos* ran around the camp and added whomever they caught.

One Sunday I went to visit a friend in the next block and was caught and put in a row of prisoners to go unload potatoes. A trainload of potatoes had just arrived in front of the camp and had to be unloaded and stored in the manner used by the farmers in eastern Europe when there was a shortage of storage buildings. I thought that this would be my last day of life, because the *kapo* supervising the work was known in the camp as "the angel of death." He was a horrible sadist who liked to kill as many prisoners as possible during the work. I had no one to help me, and to escape death in such a situation was probably impossible.

When we arrived at the train I saw what had to be done. There were large holes like graves dug in the little yard area. The potatoes had to be unloaded and put into the holes. The holes were each about five feet deep, ten feet wide, and fifty feet long. The potatoes on the top were pyramided, covered with straw, and then covered again with dirt. The holes were lined with straw on the sides and bottom before the potatoes were put in, to prevent water from coming in contact with the potatoes.

The *kapo* asked if anyone were familiar with this kind of work. I told him that I knew what had to be done because my father was a farmer and I had helped him to do the same thing every year. He ordered me to take care of the preparation of the holes. It was my job to decide how thick the layer of straw should be made on the sides and bottom of the holes and on the tops of the pyramids of potatoes. I was also to decide what form the pyramids should take and how they should be covered. This was unexpectedly good for me because I only had to run from one place to another giving instruction in how to do the work and correcting mistakes. The *kapo* and his helpers accepted me as a specialist and, although I was not a part of the administration, I was not submitted to persecution since this was not a permanent *kommando*.

While watching the progress of the work, I had opportunity to observe what was going on. What was happening was a documentary of how brutal a human being can be. The work was hard. There were wooden boxes which the prisoners had to fill with about fifty kilograms of potatoes. Then two prisoners had to carry the box by handles on each end in a running tempo to the place it was to be unloaded. Then they had to run back to the train and refill the box and repeat the procedure. The *kapo* and *forarbeiters* were angry because they had to work on Sunday and took revenge by torturing the prisoners. Many of the Polish prisoners took advantage of the fact that not all the *forarbeiters* had a stripe on their uniforms with the inscription *"forarbeiter"* on it. It was generally thought that one who was kicking and striking another was a *forarbeiter*. When a *kommando* had been formed for only a day, as in this case, it was almost impossible to tell who the *forarbeiters* were. So, some of the Polish prisoners pretended to be *forarbeiters* to escape the persecution themselves. They set up a line through which the prisoners had to run and filled it with self-styled *forarbeiters* who kicked and beat the other prisoners. The SS guards with their dogs watched the prisoners from the four corners of the area.

The Jewish prisoners were in an especially bad position since the double triangle on their uniforms prevented them from pretending to be *forarbeiters* since no Jews were allowed in the administration. They were the first to fall victims to persecution. The prisoners running with the boxes of potatoes also could not escape the persecution because there were tormentors on all sides. If they tried to escape from one, there were always the SS guards and their dogs.

When we returned from this work, of the six hundred men chosen for their strength, there were only four hundred left alive. We brought two hundred back dead. At least three-quarters of those who were still able to walk were smeared from top to bottom with their own blood.

When we came through the gate to the main camp, the orchestra was waiting and started to play a beautiful march. The column of prisoners, living skeletons smeared with blood and carrying the dead skeletons also smeared with blood, tried to keep the rhythm of the march. It was a scene far worse than anything imagined by Dante.

Chapter 11

BANDERA GRUPPE

The Ukrainian Red Cross in Krakow continued to help the Ukrainian political prisoners, but only those who were in prisons. When prisoners were sent to concentration camps, the Ukrainian Red Cross was no longer permitted to help. The attempts of the Red Cross at interventions were always met with the same answer. The Red Cross could work only in the general government, and the concentration camps were in the Reich and therefore off limits to the Red Cross territorially. However, there were some members of the Ukrainian underground movement in the Red Cross, and they never stopped looking for ways to help us, especially after they received the letter describing the actual conditions in Auschwitz.

After about four months, they were able to find a member of the Gestapo who had a special job. When there was an investigation to be made, it was given to a specialist in the Gestapo called the *sachbearbeiter*. He, with the help of a clerk, was responsible for making the investigation, writing the report, and making the recommendation as to what was to be done with the prisoner or group of prisoners in question. There was among the members of the Ukrainian underground a Dr. Mostovych who had been born around the same time and in the same village as one of the German colonists in the Ukraine, Mr. Stark. Mr. Stark, as a *Volksdeutsch*, had become a member of the Gestapo after the war started. Dr. Mostovych and Mr. Stark had been good friends in elementary school and in the gymnasium, and even after the war started, Dr. Mostovych met the German boy from Ukraine in Berlin where Dr. Mostovych had gone as a refugee. Mr. Stark was friendly even at that time. Therefore the Red Cross appealed to Herr Stark to help his friend Dr. Mostovych and the other Ukrainians among whom Herr Stark had been born and raised. Along with the appeal to his human kindness, much gold was sent to him. All Germans, even those in Hitler's administration, were very fond of gold. As a result of this appeal and the bribery, the *sachbearbeiter* agreed to do what he could to help the Ukrainians. Of course, he couldn't do anything important, but he could make some changes in our situation in the concentration camp.

In December, 1942 when Dr. Mostovych and some other members of the underground were to be transferred to Auschwitz, Herr Stark came with them as *sachbearbeiter* in the Ukrainian affair.

Our group was called Bandera *Gruppe* and on all our personal documents this name appeared. The name was taken from the family name of the leader of our organization, Stepan Bandera, who was himself held in the concentration camp in Sachsenhausen near Berlin.

Reporting the transfer of the new prisoners, the *sachbearbeiter* explained to the officer in Auschwitz that the Gestapo would like all Ukrainians to be held in one room so that when a decision was made regarding their case they would all be together for any action to be taken. This was something new for Auschwitz, although the rest of the concentration camps had long ago started dividing prisoners by nationality. In Birkenau there were divisions for Jews, Gypsies, and so forth, but there was no division by nationality in the main camp. The Ukrainians belonged to many different *kommandos* and lived in different blocks. The administration accepted the order without question and made a list of all the members of the Bandera *Gruppe*. After night roll call we were transferred to a room in Block 17.

We were also fortunate enough to find a place to work together. A group of prisoners who had been working in the kitchen as potato peelers were transferred to another camp.

We immediately contacted the *kapo* of the potato peelers and, through bribery, made an agreement with him that we would be taken into the kitchen as potato peelers. So now we not only lived together, but worked together also.

This was considered good work and it was not easy to be chosen for it. *Volksdeutsch* Poles who were chosen to be *kapos* and *unterkapos* in this work tried to preserve it for members of the Polish aristocracy who came into the concentration camp. Therefore most of the prisoners working here were politicians, ranking military men, or nobility.

In a long room close to the kitchen, about three hundred prisoners worked at peeling potatoes. They were divided into groups of twelve, each group sitting around a table working for ten hours. This was, of course, much easier than working outside in the streets or on the buildings because here one only had to keep up the tempo of the peeling to satisfy the *kapos* and *forarbeiters*. Because the *kapos* and *forarbeiters* were friends of most of the prisoners working here, they did very little persecution.

The soup that the prisoners ate each day consisted mainly of potatoes, so this group had to peel enough potatoes each day for the twenty thousand or so prisoners in the main camp and the one thousand SS men living in the SS barracks close to the main camp. Potato peelers also had to prepare all other kinds of vegetables for the kitchen for the soup for the SS men. Therefore it was often possible to steal a carrot, some cabbage, or other vegetable, and conceal it in the pocket until one could go to the nearby toilet and consume it.

The next room was used for the barrels of soup ready to be distributed to the prisoners and for storage of the empty barrels as they were brought back. Prisoners among the potato peelers who had friends in the kitchen would arrange for them to leave one full barrel of soup among the empty ones. When the potato peelers had to help with the moving of the empty barrels, they would manage to take the full barrel into the toilet. Then members of this group of prisoners would, one by one, go into the toilet and get part of the soup. Sometimes there was also opportunity to "organize" bread or margerine and consume that in the toilet.

Since the prisoners transferred from the kitchen were taken from many groups we were quite spread out. The Polish prisoners in the groups accepted us with distrust at first. They thought we were agents of the Gestapo sent to listen to their conversations. They soon saw that their suspicions had no basis, and since most of the prisoners working here were intelligent people, relations between the prisoners working in the potato-peeling *kommando* soon became friendly.

There were among the Polish prisoners many politicians and many of them were eager to discuss political problems. In the group next to me there was Cirankiewich, a leading member of the Polish Socialists, who, after surviving the war in the concentration camp, became President of the Communist Polish Republic.

Of course, I took advantage of every opportunity to organize additional portions of bread, soup, or other food. As a result, after a few weeks in the kitchen, I felt that I was no longer a *musulman*; I could again walk normally. Then came the day when I had the chance to feel the pleasure of fighting back.

From the beginning I had been especially depressed by the prisoners' inability to fight back. We had to endure any humiliation and persecution by any member of the administration. We had to suffer without any attempt to defend ourselves because we were too weak. Any such attempt in this place where there were no protective laws would have meant our immediate death.

One day while I was peeling potatoes I consumed too much cabbage and my stomach revolted. I couldn't go to the toilet in our block because, as I have mentioned, it was used for hiding and consuming food. I decided to go to the next block. This was not as simple as it might sound because the prisoners were not permitted to enter the blocks and use the toilets during the day. There was a prisoner called a *scheismeister*, responsible for cleaning the toilets, who watched that no one came in during the day. I did not expect him to be there, and when I had just taken my place in the toilet, he came in and hit me with his fist. Deciding in a moment that I was no longer a *musulman*, I decided to fight back. I jumped up and caught him with my arm and forearm in the so-called "half-nelson." He was very surprised and though he was much bigger and stronger than I, I managed to force his head into the hole for the toilet and he was unable to remove it. He shouted horribly, and I took advantage of his position to hit and kick him a dozen or so times before I escaped back to the kitchen. It was about ten minutes before anyone came to help him remove his head from the hole. He explained what had happened, so they came looking for the prisoner who had done this. Finally they came to the room where we were working. We were ordered to stand in rows and the *scheismeister* tried to find the one who had hit him. I was afraid because I knew that if he recognized me, it would be the last day of my life. Fortunately, he and the other guards didn't even look in the section where I was standing because none of us looked physically capable of doing what had been done. They were looking for a tall young prisoner and since there were none here, they decided that it was probably someone from another *kommando* and left. I had never felt such satisfaction as I did then from knowing that I was not totally helpless and could sometimes protect myself.

After our group had been put together in one room in Block 17, we persuaded the *blockältester* that the *stubendienst* should be one of us. We told him that this would prevent arguments between the *stubendienst* and others in the room. The *blockältester,* a German criminal, agreed. (He was especially impressed by our promise that we would provide him with a pack of cigarettes every day if he would grant our request.) This gave us a kind of autonomy. Having the *stubendienst* one of us meant that at least for the night we were free from additional persecution by the camp administration.

Shortly after that, the camp *kommandant* found out that there was a group of Ukrainians living in the camp and he was anxious to find out who we were. He ordered our *stubendienst* to report to him. We were afraid that all our newfound advantages would be lost, he would not approve of the arrangements that had been made. Unexpectedly, however, the conference had a happy ending.

In the camp at that time there was only one official interpreter, a member of an aristocratic Polish-German family of the former Austro-Hungarian Empire. He was from Bukovina and was, therefore, fluent in Ukrainian as well as German and Polish. He had studied at an English university and was working for an English newspaper at the time he was sent to Auschwitz.

Our *stubendienst* was a young lawyer fluent in German. Nevertheless, the *kommandant* chose to respect the regulation requiring the presence of an interpreter. Our room elder, Mr. Rak, was not allowed to answer the *kommandant* directly in German, but had to wait for the interpreter to translate what the *kommandant* had said into Ukrainian, give his answer in Ukrainian, and let the interpreter translate the answer into German for the *kommandant.* When Mr. Rak was asked who the members of the Bandera *Gruppe* were, he replied that we were former members of the Ukrainian underground movement who had fought for the independence of Ukraine during the Polish and Russian occupations. He was surprised, then, to hear the interpreter translating his answer as, "We are members of a group who think the best solution for the Ukraine is to have a German king. Before the war began we wanted to have a Hapsburg king, but since the Hapsburgs no longer exist, we would like to have a king from the family of the last German king." Mr. Rak protested, but the interpreter warned him in Ukrainian to be silent and he was dismissed.

After roll call that night, the interpreter visited us in our room and explained why he had translated the answer that way. He told us that he was half-Ukrainian; his mother was Ukrainian. Therefore he had grown up among Ukrainians and had sympathy for us. From working with the *kommandant* every day, he had learned that the *kommandant*, before joining the NSDAP, had been a German monarchist and still favored a monarchy. He had told the interpreter that since Germany was going to become a world empire, in his opinion, it would be best for Germany to have a king for ceremonial purposes; the Führer would still be the real leader. That is why the interpreter had told the *kommandant* that we favored a German king. On the top of our papers in the *Politische Abteilung* there was a notation that we were Ukrainian Communists. Thus a number of designations were applied to the members of the Organization of Ukrainian Nationalists—to the *kommandant* we were Ukrainian monarchists; on order of the administration we were Polish, Russian, or Czech; and to the *Politische Abteilung*, we were Communists.

Now since the room elder who checked the stripes with our numbers during Sunday inspection was one of us and the *blockältester* was being paid a pack of cigarettes every day not to interfere, we decided to change our triangles and put a "U" on all of them.

One day after we had changed the letters I was peeling potatoes and one of the Polish prisoners noticed the "U." Intending to make a joke, he said, "How are you, sir, from Uruguay? I see that you are from Uruguay by the 'U' on your strip." All the Polish prisoners began to laugh.

I answered him quietly, "I feel the same as you, neighbor."

"What do you mean by calling me 'neighbor?' " he asked. "I am not your neighbor."

"If my 'U' refers to Uruguay, then your 'P' must mean Paraguay. You and I are neighbors," I replied.

The Polish prisoners didn't mention the letter on our uniforms again.

The kitchen had to prepare food for the prisoners as well as for the SS living in the barracks just outside the main camp. The soup for the guards was delivered by the prisoners under the control of the SS men. One day I was ordered to be a part of the group delivering the barrels. When the work was finished and we were returning to the kitchen, the guard escorting us came only as far as the gate, reported that we were back, and left us. The foreman in charge of our group reported to another SS guard that there were twelve men coming back from delivering the soup. He had made a mistake in using the word *men* instead of *prisoners*. The guard, not caring that the foreman was himself a German, jumped him like an angry tiger and hit and kicked him all the while shouting angrily, "What are you saying, you idiot? Don't you know there are no men in prison? Here are only numbers, prisoners."

"Jawohl, Herr Scharführer—twelve *prisoners,"* corrected the foreman, glad that the SS guard was satisfied with hitting and kicking him only once.

Chapter 12

IN THE EFFEKTENKAMMER

The first six months of our imprisonment in Auschwitz were coming to an end. The day we had been brought here we had not believed that we could survive three days. After we had survived the three days, we wondered if we could survive three weeks. The majority of us were still alive. The first three weeks had been the worst and had taken a big toll. Seven of the first group of twenty-five had lost their lives during this time.

It was getting close to Christmas, which, according to Ukrainian custom, was celebrated on January 6 and 7. Christmas Eve is especially important to Ukrainians. Since we were living in comparatively better circumstances than when we had arrived, we decided to organize a Christmas Eve supper. Our friends working in the kitchen prepared a traditional supper—Ukrainian borsch and *kutia*. We waited impatiently for the January 6 evening roll call to come to an end. Unexpectedly, at the end of the roll call, came the order, *"Alle Ukrainer antreten."* This meant that after dismissal, all the Ukrainians were to take places in front of the kitchen. The prisoners were dismissed and we gathered in front of the kitchen. We were shocked to find out how many Ukrainians there actually were in the camp. Our group, arrested in September, 1941, consisted of fewer than fifty at that time, but we knew there were many other Ukrainians arrested for different reasons. Some were even members of our group but had been arrested separately and had denied that they were members of the underground, preferring to be listed as Polish or Russian. Some had refused to work in Germany, some were suspected of aiding the Ukrainian resistance and others were village mayors who had not fulfilled their obligation of confiscating corn and other things from the peasants for delivery to the Germans. We knew all this because we had met some of them from time to time, but we had no idea that there were this many—more than one thousand Ukrainian prisoners. Some wore "P," some "R," and even some "C." These ("C" for Czech) had lived in a small part of Ukraine which, during the time between World Wars I and II, had belonged to the Czechoslovakian Republic. Our group took places at the end of a long column. No one knew why we had been ordered here and so there were pessimistic and optimistic explanations. The optimists thought that the Ukrainian Red Cross had finally received permission to send packages and, since it was Ukrainian Christmas, we would receive a package. The pessimists were of a different opinion. They thought we would be asked one by one if we preferred to join the German Auxiliary Army or stay here.

In front of the column, just in front of the Gestapo office, there was a small group of about fifty prisoners and a group of SS officers, a *lagerkommandant*, a *lagerführer*, an *arbeitsführer* and someone else. The prisoners in that group were interrogated one by one. We could see from the end of the column what was happening, but we couldn't hear anything that was being said. We were confused by the various reactions to the prisoners' answers. One prisoner, after he had answered, would be hit in the face just once. Another would not be hit at all. A third would be severely beaten, kicked, and pushed aside. This was the largest group. We tried to figure out what was happening. One decided that, as he had thought, we were being asked to join the German army. When a prisoner agreed, he was sent to the first group without any beating; those who were unsure would be hit in the face and sent to another group until they had made a decision; those who refused would be beaten and returned to the camp or perhaps sent to Block 11 for execution. After about twenty of our group had been questioned, we were all dismissed. We returned to our room and began our Christmas supper. Shortly the interpreter joined us and explained what had been happening. He said that there was a special *kommando* in camp called the *effektenkammer* which worked with the belongings of the prisoners. When prisoners were brought to Birkenau they had to put all their possessions on a part of Birkenau's courtyard called "the Canada." Prisoners brought to the main camp were ordered to undress and place all clothing in a paper bag. The number the prisoner received was placed on the bag which was disinfected and stored in a big room. If the prisoner was later freed, all his belongings had to be returned to him. Seldom was anything returned because the only prisoners who were ever released, and then only extremely rarely, were usually German political prisoners. In such cases, the prisoner was taken to a room where he was fed double portions of the soup made for the SS men until he looked strong and healthy. Then he was taken to a place and allowed to select clothing from a stockpile so that he would make a good impression on the people who would meet him immediately after his release from the concentration camp. Nevertheless, the cataloging procedure had been continued.

The work in the *effektenkammer* was considered a prominent job because it was under a roof and comparatively quiet. Therefore, the German political prisoners and Polish prominents sought these jobs. Most of them were from Silesia, the territory where the camp was located. Many of the new prisoners brought gold pieces and when they were taken away, the prisoners working in the *effektenkammer* tried to smuggle them to the civilians through other prisoners working outside the camp in industry. This practice had been discovered and a special investigation was ordered. The investigation was what had been taking place in front of the columns of assembled Ukrainian prisoners. The Germans were put aside for further investigation into how far they had become involved in the smuggling. The *Volksdeutsch* were hit in the face and the Polish prisoners were immediately beaten and taken to Block 11 for execution.

Prior to the investigation, the smuggling was discussed by the administration and one of the SS guards suggested that it might be good to replace these prisoners with Ukrainians because the Ukrainians had a good reputation in regard to criminal activity. Also, he reasoned, since the population around the camp was Polish, it would be unlikely that they would cooperate with the Ukrainian prisoners in such a dangerous undertaking. The *lagerführer* agreed, and that was the reason the Ukrainian prisoners had all been ordered to report together. So the fifty prisoners at the beginning of the column had their numbers put on a list and were ordered to report to the *effektenkammer*, Block 24. Since our group had been at the end of the column, the selection process didn't reach us and that is why we didn't know what was happening. Anyway, we were happy that our fears had been unfounded, and we proceeded with our celebration—a simple Ukrainian Christmas.

The *effektenkammer* was located next to the kitchen block. Therefore, the guards who had to inspect the *effektenkammer* often came to the kitchen on the pretense of visiting their friends (the guards in charge of our *kommando*), but actually to steal food. A few days after the Ukrainians had been assigned to the *effektenkammer kommando*, a guard came to the kitchen and began to complain about the members of the *kommando* to his friend. He said that they were unable to do the work they were assigned and that he was disappointed in what he had heard about Ukrainians. They were, according to him, half-illiterate and he didn't know what to do since they were assigned to him by the *lagerführer*. He was afraid to complain. The problem was that the fifty selected all happened to be from eastern Ukraine and had had only an elementary education. They knew nothing of the Latin alphabet, and the only languages they knew were Ukrainian and Russian. Now when they were put in the offices and required to register French and Belgian prisoners they were not able even to catch the prisoner's name, much less ask the required questions. The *kapo* of our *kommando* said that he couldn't understand why this was so, because in his *kommando* there was a group of Ukrainians who were all highly educated and fluent in German.

They decided to make an exchange and we were put into

a line and taken to the *effektenkammer* to replace the others. They were taken to the potato peeling department. Both groups were happy with the exchange because, although there was no longer the possibility of organizing food in the *effektenkammer*, the work was even better because it was in an office; the other group was equally as happy to be able to work in the kitchen where they could so easily "organize" food.

The purpose of the *effektenkammer*, as mentioned earlier, was the registration and storage of the clothing and personal belongings of the prisoners. The theory was that everything a prisoner had must be put in storage for him. When a prisoner died his number was reported to the *effektenkammer*. If he was a German, his belongings were sent to his family. Otherwise the best pieces of clothing were kept for the rare cases in which a prisoner was released. The rest was distributed to the German civilian population.

The *kommando* was subdivided into many small departments. One group had to make a list consisting of the prisoner's name, his number, and all the articles he had brought with him. When the prisoner was undressed, his clothes were put in a plastic bag with his number, and another section of the *effektenkammer* took it for disinfection. After the disinfection process, another section of the *effektenkammer* took the bag for storage in the storage room.

Since the population of the prison averaged about twenty thousand, there were about that many bags in the storage room. Many prisoners, therefore, were kept busy bringing new bags for storage and disposing of the bags of prisoners who had died.

When we came to the *effektenkammer* we were divided into the *sub-kommandos* at random. The first group was sent to the office. I was not among them, but worked in the storage room. It was better work than cleaning the streets and far better than the construction work, but it was, nevertheless, manual labor. Fortunately, the *kapo* of this section was a *Volksdeutsch*, a Polish-German boy, who had been the best player on the soccer team before the war. He was a real *Volksdeutsch* because his sister was married to a German general. Although he privately regarded himself as Polish, he was registered as

German. Through the efforts of his brother-in-law he was released from the concentration camp a few weeks later. At the time we came to his *kommando*, he was waiting for release. He had been a university student before he was arrested, so he liked to hear my stories about the personal lives of Hitler, Mussolini, Goering, and so on. From time to time, he would call me to his office and talk about these things. He received an additional portion of bread and coffee which he shared with me. When, after three weeks, he was freed, he first sent me to work in the *disinfectionkammer*, where the clothes were brought for the disinfection process.

The work in disinfection was divided into two shifts of twelve hours each. One week we worked twelve hours during the day and the next week we worked twelve hours during the night. Eight of us worked on each shift. We sorted all the clothing and removed papers and anything else that would be dangerous when put in the very hot chamber. Each piece of clothing was put on a separate hanger and placed in a very high-temperature chamber for thirty minutes. It was then taken from the hangers and put back into the prisoners' bags.

The work in this *kommando* was convenient, especially during the night shift. Between the time the disinfection chamber was loaded and the time it had to be unloaded, there was about thirty minutes during which the prisoners could talk, read, or simply relax. The things that came from the disinfection chamber were especially evil-smelling, so the guards rarely came for inspection. We had much freedom compared to the other *kommandos*.

One of the prisoners who worked on the same shift with me was a very interesting person. He was a German religious prisoner, a Jehovah's Witness. Because he was German he was entitled to be a boss, a *kapo*, but because of his religion he refused, preferring to be a simple worker. He had been sent to this *kommando*. During the night shift we had the opportunity to talk about many things. He told me what had happened when he was first brought to camp.

A trainload of Jewish people who were being transported to the concentration camp came to the town where he was living. They were in miserable circumstances and begged, through the windows of the train, for someone to help them with bread or water. He brought them some bread and water and a guard saw him. The guard pushed him into the train, not caring who he was, and he was thus brought to Auschwitz as a Jewish prisoner. He did not protest because he felt whatever happened was God's will for him.

When the transport was taken from the train and lined up at Birkenau, he was chosen for the *sonderkommando* because he was young and strong. As a member of the *kommando* he had much opportunity to see what was going on there. It was from him that I received a firsthand report about the gassing of the Jewish prisoners at Birkenau.

The *sonderkommando*, according to Martin, the Jehovah's Witness, consisted of about six hundred prisoners selected from Jewish transports. The prisoners were chosen for their youth and bodily strength and good physical condition. They were not given regular prison dress, but were given civilian clothing marked with a red stripe from the top to the bottom of the back of the coat and on on both sides of the pants. Their prisoner number was marked on the front and back in big numerals. No triangle or nationality letter was used because normally, they were all Jewish. They received plenty of good food like that prepared for the guards and even, from time to time, were given a drink. They worked in the gas chambers and crematoria for three or four months. Then one day they would all be taken to the gas chambers and executed themselves and replaced with a new set of prisoners. A list of the members of the *sonderkommando* was made by numbers and there were not any questions made into their personalities. Therefore, there was no way for anyone to know that Martin was a German, not a Jew.

When a new transport was brought into Birkenau and unloaded, the *sonderkommando* was already waiting with three buses bearing the sign of the International Red Cross. A Jewish physician was present to make the impression on the prisoners that there really was medical help available. First of all, all babies and small children were taken from their mothers. Their parents were told that they had been taken to a hospital, but they were actually all taken to the crematoria. They were undressed and put on the iron bars alive and sent into the crematoria. After a few minutes they were all cremated.

In the other cars with the sign of the International Red Cross, bottles of poison gas were brought to the gas chambers. The prisoners were divided into two groups—one of men and one of women—and were ordered to undress and go into the shower room (actually the gas chamber). When the room was filled with prisoners, the doors were locked and the gas was let in through the shower openings. After about ten minutes, all in the room would be dead. The doors were opened and the corpses were taken to the crematoria for cremation by the members of the *sonderkommando*.

Although four crematoria were in operation twenty-four hours each day, it was necessary to have, in addition, two piles for cremation of corpses.

The old and sick were treated like the babies and children because they could make trouble going into the gas chambers. They were put in the car with the Red Cross insignia and told they were being taken to the hospital. They were given an injection of poison, which they were told was medicine against the epidemic. After just a few minutes they would all be dead and would be taken to the crematoria.

Before the corpses were cremated, they had to be carefully checked by the members of the *sonderkommando* for gold teeth. All these gold teeth had to be removed and collected. Among the Jewish people there were large numbers of gold teeth, so this was considered a good way to collect the high-priced gold. Also, all the corpses had to be shaved because the hair, too, was being collected.

One night Martin told me a macabre story about a member of the *sonderkommando* called "Crazy Izak." He had witnessed this while he was a member of the *sonderkommando*.

Izak, while a young student, had fallen in love with a classmate, a Jewish girl named Rosa. She categorically refused his advances and instead married a German boy. In many cases it was not easy to find out that a family had a Jewish background, and so it was in Rosa's case. She pretended to be a German, and so there was no danger for her.

Shortly after that, Izak was arrested and brought to the concentration camp. He didn't forget her. He was chosen to work in the *sonderkommando* and when he, as all others, was told to write letters to relatives and friends, he wrote to Rosa. He told her in his letter that he was glad that she had managed to hide the fact that she was a Jewess and would be able to remain alive. Of course, these letters were censored and the clerk who read Izak's letter reported that he had discovered a German lady of Jewish descent. The report was investigated. When it was confirmed, both the lady and her husband were arrested. He was sent to the main camp and she was added to a transport from her town to Auschwitz.

Izak waited for the transport from his town. As a member of the *sonderkommando*, he had the opportunity to check all the prisoners coming off the railroad cars. Finally Rosa arrived. She was horrified because she didn't know what was going to happen to her. Izak told her that he would try to help her because he loved her. She told him that he was crazy, that she was married, and they could not talk about love in such a situation. He continued to talk to her and urged her to remain close to the wall when she entered the shower room. He told her that immediately after the doors were opened she would be taken to another room in the camp and he would be able to help her there.

She did as he asked and when the door to the gas chamber was opened after about fifteen minutes, Izak was the first to jump into the room. He picked up Rosa's corpse, probably still warm, and ran with her to his room, shouting that she was his. The members of the *sonderkommando* and the guards were shocked. The guards, nevertheless, said to leave him alone for a while before he would go after her for the crematorium.

In addition to the crematoria there were, as I have mentioned two piles for burning corpses. In the area of these piles worked the so-called "Department of Herr Molle." In the main camp it was *Hauptschaarführer* Palitsch who found special pleasure in killing scores of prisoners every morning in the courtyard of Block 11 with his needle gun. Here was another sadist like him, a member of the guards, *Oberschaarführer* Molle. It was not clear to Martin what principle was used in selecting the victims, but every day about fifty or a hundred prisoners were not sent to the gas chambers but were brought to a room which had one of its doors facing the pyre. The prisoners, one by one, were ordered to enter the room and totally undress. The prisoner was then told to leave the room so he could be replaced by another prisoner. When he went out, the *oberschaarführer* and another SS would be waiting for him. A few yards away would be two members of the *sonder-kommando*. They would catch the prisoner by his hands and arms and force him to kneel. Then Molle would shoot him in the head. It made no difference whether the victim was dead or not. He was thrown into the flames of the pyre and replaced by another. So, one by one, the group would be liquidated.

One day Martin was selected for the work with *Oberschaarführer* Molle and it happened that the guard with the group was an old school friend of Martin's. He was shocked to see Martin and asked him what he was doing there. When Martin had explained to him what had happened, the guard took him to the Gestapo office. After some confusion, it was decided to register him as a religious prisoner. He received a violet triangle and was sent to the main camp. Here, as I have said, he refused to accept a position as boss and was sent to work in the *effektenkammer*.

Everything he saw he accepted without comment because of his religious beliefs. He was a Jehovah's Witness and his opinion about what was happening in the world, and especially here, he explained to me in the following way: He said that the Lord had created the world and everything was perfect. It was easy at that time to decide what should be done and what should not be done. One of the angels decided one day that he could arrange everything even better than the Lord had done. His name was Satan. The Lord knew that. He could send for the offending angel Satan and put him in a concentration camp and that would be the end of it, but He also knew that some people then might think that Satan was, perhaps, right. So the Lord decided to do something else. He sent for Satan and told him that if he thought he could do everything better, he could try ruling the world. That, according to Martin, was the reason that everything was in such confusion. No one knew under Satan's rule what was just and what was unjust. The just suffered and the unjust were rewarded. Hitler and Mussolini were not really human beings; they were agents of Satan and did what he told them to do. He said that one day God would call all people for final judgment and ask them if they had liked Satan's rule, if they thought that Satan had done a better job of ordering the world than He had done. Of course, everyone would acknowledge God as the only Lord and then everything would again be arranged perfectly and Satan with his helpers, the devils, would be sent to a concentration camp. Martin said that it was not an accident that he, a pure German, was arrested, made a member of the *sonderkommando*, recognized by a classmate, and sent to the main camp after three weeks. He said all this had happened because the Lord wanted to have a witness to the happenings in a concentration camp organized by the Nazis.

Martin was a good friend and I liked him very much, but he liked to eat and soon found that it would be better for him to work in the kitchen. It was no problem for him to arrange it because of his nationality. He was transferred to the kitchen and I could no longer meet him as often as when we worked together in the disinfection department.

I asked him not to forget that I was still alive when he was transferred to the kitchen *kommando*. I asked him to try to bring me something good to eat once in a while. In return, I would be a witness, if I survived, that he was a good and honest man, even though he was of 100 percent German background. He smiled at this and did try to help me.

Staszek, who replaced Martin in my *kommando*, was a young Polish boy from Warsaw. He was a former student and officer in the Polish army, the son of a rich physician. During the nights we had long discussions about Ukrainian-Polish relations because, living far from the Ukrainian territory occupied by Poland, all he knew about the Ukraine was what he had learned from the Polish chauvinistic newspapers. He thought that Ukrainians were Mongolian, almost all illiterate, and born hating Polish people, who, in his opinion, were especially intelligent and more civilized. Now he was confused because he couldn't deny the fact that most of the Ukrainians working in the *effektenkammer*, among them myself, had a higher education. I even knew the literary Polish language better than he himself did.

One day he gave me the opportunity to see what a chauvinistic education really means. In the discussion I recited a prayer and gave the content of what I wanted to recite, adding that I was not sure exactly how it was said in Polish. He asked me what I meant by saying that I was Ukrainian. If I were Catholic I had to pray in Polish was what he told me. I told him that he was mistaken, that I was praying in Ukrainian. He said that it was not possible to pray to the Lord's mother in Ukrainian because she, as everyone knew, was a queen of Poland and understood only Polish. I thought that he was joking, but I found out that he had been taught so as a small child. At twenty-four he still believed this to be true. In spite of his shocking chauvinism he liked me and we remained friends.

Another prisoner who worked with me and soon became my close friend was Franek, a former member of the Polish parliament and a leading member of the Polish Socialist Party. He was from Silesia which was now, after the occupation of Poland, a part of Germany. Because of that he told me that for the Germans he was a pure German and for the Polish he was a Pole. He liked political discussions not only of theory but also of the present situation. He was not very strong in geography, especially political geography. He had connection with some other German prisoners who had access to a secret radio and gathered information from English and French broadcasts. Franek collected this information, put the names of places where the battles were occurring on a piece of paper, and then brought them to me to find out where the places were and what the battles meant. He wanted to know how far these places were from Auschwitz, how long I thought the American or English armies from the west or the Russian army from the east would take to reach Auschwitz, and when the war would be over.

As a German, he was entitled to receive, legally and normally, a German newspaper, *Volkischer Beobachter*. Because he brought his copy to work, which was not officially permitted, I now had the opportunity to read a regular newspaper. From his reports and this newspaper, I arranged a news report for the other members of our group in the room each night, and gave them the news about miltary and political events outside the camp.

The work in *effektenkammer* was relatively tolerable. The

general situation in Auschwitz in 1944 started to change for the better. This raised my hope for surviving. No special danger to my life was now evident.

But unexpectedly one day, after the roll call, a group of prisoners was ordered to report for transport to another camp, to a quarry. I was among them. This was an extremely serious danger, because it was well known that no prisoner could survive there. Immediately after the roll call I went to my friends, one after another, but no one could help. The next day, at 10 A.M., all the members of the group had to report and be transported.

All night I thought about what to do.

In the morning I asked the *stubendienst* for the knife he used for cutting bread, to cut my piece of bread. I took it and the next moment my palm was badly slashed. The blood spurted like a fountain. I was taken to the hospital where more than a dozen stitches were required for the wound.

At 10 A.M., I dutifully reported for transport. There was a physician there to check if each prisoner selected was fit for work. When he saw my badly bleeding and stiched-up hand, he ordered my number crossed off the list, and sent me to the hospital.

Chapter 13

NEUE WÄSCHEREI

After two days in the *krankenbau*, the hospital, I had to go back to work. Since my place in the *effektenkammer* was already filled by another prisoner I had to look for a new *kommando*. During the time I was in the *krankenbau* I was looking for this work, and using my connections, I found work in *neue wäscherei*, the laundry. It was called *neue*, the new, because the laundry was at first in the wooden barrack, between Blocks 1 and 2, occupying half the space of the barrack. Now a new building had been built in front of Block 11 and was totally occupied by the laundry. Here the clothing, not only of the prisoners but also of the SS and the five thousand air force men stationed not far from the camp, were taken care of. Most of the work was for the SS and the air force, because we usually had to clean just the prisoners' shirts. The prisoners had no linen and no pants. It was told that the prisoners received what they needed once a week, but really only the prominents got everything.

Since the clothing was counted and distributed according to the report from roll call, the prominents were often able to take two or three shirts for themselves, leaving the *musulmans* with only one of the worst shirts each month.

The work was similar to that which I performed in the disinfection department of the *effektenkammer*. There were five very large washing machines in the room. The prisoner work-

ing at each machine had to load one hundred pieces of clothing in the machine, add soap and other chemicals, wait
thirty minutes, and unload the machine. It took one hour for
each round. We worked on twelve-hour shifts. One week we
worked twelve hours during the day and the next week we
would work twelve hours during the night.

In the next room were the machines for ironing. Everything that was washed for the SS guards and the air force
men had to be nicely ironed.

I worked on the washing machines. My helper and the
eight others working on the same shift were Jewish prisoners.
Some were from Germany, one was from Holland, and one
was from Lithuania. One of the Germans was the youngest
brother of the German writer Stefan Zweig.

During the nightshift there was plenty of time for discussion, because the SS guard who came to check was always
fed by the *kapo* and left to sleep in the *kapo's* office. If
another SS came, or if there was any trouble, he had to be
awakened. Otherwise, he wasn't around. After we had loaded
our machines, we had thirty minutes for discussion.

The prisoners working here were interesting personalities.
The brother of Stefan Zweig was a nice-looking young man of
about 19 or 20 years. He had been a student of the university
in Berlin. He was called *"Hochstapler"* by the other Jewish
prisoners. This means "Pretender." This was because he pretended to be a member of the aristocracy and highly educated. On the other hand his fellow prisoners had found out
that he was extremely poor in Jewish history and religion. His
older brother had managed to leave Germany before the beginning of the arrests of the Jewish people. The other members of the family pretended to be Germans. It was not easy
in Germany to find out who had a Jewish background, but he
was finally discovered and arrested by the police. During the
interrogation, he gave the address of his sister who was married to a German army officer. As a result, both his sister and
his brother-in-law were arrested and sent to concentration
camps. Because Zweig's brother-in-law was a German, he
found for himself a good position here in Auschwitz. Therefore, knowing the situation, we expected that when he found
his brother-in-law, the youngest Zweig, he would take re-

venge for causing the death of his wife and his arrest. On the contrary, he took no revenge at all and instead helped the young Zweig by putting him in a good kommando and coming to see him from time to time to bring him bread.

Another Jewish prisoner, who was about 40 years old, was a leading member of the Communist party in Holland. He was called Karl, but I suspect that was a nickname because he often cited Karl Marx during discussions. It was dangerous to cite Marx in the concentration camps then, so when he talked, he would only say "Karl had said," or "Karl had written," or "according to Karl." He was a very intelligent man and we spent many nights in the discussion of communism, socialism, and other political ideologies. I explained the ideology of the Ukrainian underground movement. When I told him that although we were called nationalists, we advocated freedom for all nations and individuals, he told me that we were really communists. We should, therefore, change our name to communists. I told him that we were not communists. I explained about the political and personal persecution we had suffered under the Russian government who pretended to be the only real Marxists. Karl said that Russians are not real communists; they were only pretending. He said that real communism as he understood it was the same as the ideology of the Ukrainian underground movement. We became friends respecting the political opinions of each other.

The most colorful figure here was Jakob. He was about 45 years old and was a tall, strong, Spanish Jew. He was a former commissioned officer in the Spanish Republican Army which had fought against Franco. After the war was over, he had retreated with others to France. When France was occupied by Germany, he was put into prison, then brought here. He, according to his political affiliation, was an anarchist. He liked to take part in our discussions, and when Karl and I would talk about a sick situation and decide that it was very difficult to find the proper solution to many problems, he would offer a simple panacea, which he called the anarchistic solution to the problem. I said that everyone should be permitted to live as he wanted, because no one is entitled to kill or persecute another. He said that people should live their lives as brothers, but they should be very careful that there are no more babies born. Then, after 50 or 75 years, there would be no more problems in the world because there would be no people left alive. Thus all tragic problems would be definitely and once and forever solved. I smiled at him sarcastically and told him that while he might think he had the most intelligent solution, I thought it was stupid because only the intelligent people would apply his solution, and after fifty years there would be no more intelligent people, but billions of primitive, uneducated people who would live everywhere. He did not agree, and continued to insist that this was the best and only solution for all the problems of human beings.

More interesting to me was the illustration he provided about the psychology of the persecuted prisoners in the German concentration camps. In front of our building was the *krankenbau*. Once a week it was visited by a German physician and an SS. As I have already mentioned, all prisoners there were ordered into the corridor and were checked. When the physician found someone incurably sick, he was ordered to undress. The group of naked prisoners was put into a big truck and taken to Birkenau and gassed. The prisoners were told that there was a special section of a hospital in Birkenau for them, but all prisoners knew what it meant to be ordered to undress and get into the big truck. After the inspection of the physician was completed, the truck would take its position backed up to the staircase of the *krankenbau* with its doors open. The prisoners would file into it one by one. During this process, those of us working in the laundry were ordered to stay away from the windows, but when we saw that no one was watching us, we disregarded the order and watched to see who was going into the truck. The prisoners never revolted against this. When we discussed this interesting phenomenon, Jakob said that all these Jewish prisoners were sheep because they all went like sheep and never tried to resist. He was of the opinion that it was necessary to fight before one dies. Had it been his lot to die, he would demonstrate how a prisoner should die.

Fate made a joke of him. One day a special disease was discovered on his skin, and he was sent to the hospital. The physician was not sure what it was, and during the next inspection we watched through the windows. I was quite interested to see if Jakob would be taken to be gassed. I saw him. He was undressed, terrified, and went into the truck as quietly as all the others. Just a few days before, he had said that he would demonstrate how to die. This meant that a week of waiting and seeing the real situation had totally broken his will to resist. He, as all the others he had called sheep, submitted himself quietly and without resistance to execution.

Another prisoner, David, about 50 years old, whom the prisoners called Rabbi, was interested in Jewish religion and was glad to find out that I was familiar with Jewish history and religion and could speak Yiddish. He had managed to find a three-volume history of the Jewish people among the belongings of one of the gassed prisoners and had smuggled them to the laundry. During the night, he would take care of my machine so I could study more about the religion, customs, and history of the Jewish people.

Young Abram, who, before his arrest, was a senior in high school in Lithuania, was interested in mathematics. Often he would ask me to come to his machine and we would work out mathematical equations and other mathematical and geometrical problems on the floor with chalk.

Another young boy, Isaac, puzzled me with his voice. He was about 17 or 18, in good physical condition, normally developed, but he had no hair on his face and his voice was like that of a young girl. Soon Karl told me of Isaac's secret. When Isaac was arrested and brought to the concentration camp, he had been selected as a subject for medical experimentation. He was taken to a special section of the hospital where the German physicians were performing all kinds of experiments. On him, they tried to find the simplest method of castration. His genitalia were cut off, and after the wounds had healed, he was sent to work in the laundry. Once a week he had to be checked. The physicians were interested in what effect that simple method of castration would have on the development of a young boy. This was why his voice, after a few months, had changed and the hair on his face no longer grew.

The short and vivid Josele was called by his friends *Kachke* in Polish-Yiddish, which means duck, because he walked like a duck. He was a former simple businessman and was always busy organizing something in the laundry and smuggling it to the inhabitants of Block 10. At the end of 1943, Block 10 had been taken for a special department of medical experimentation. Here were brought young Jewish girls and medical experiments were performed on them. It was not difficult to pay the administration in the block some margarine or something and visit the girls. Josele tried to take care of them and liked to take things to them. He furnished me with a good deal of information about medical experiments performed in the main camp in Block 10 and in Birkenau.

Chapter 14

MEDICAL EXPERIMENTS IN AUSCHWITZ CONCENTRATION CAMP

All medical experiments performed on prisoners in Auschwitz were supervised by a German physician, Dr. Mengele. At the beginning, the experiments were carried out only in Birkenau, but at the end of 1943, Block 10 in the main camp was also used for experimenting with female prisoners.

This was called the *Experimenten des Higienischen Instituts,* and was under the supervision of Dr. Woehrle. In both places, especially in Birkenau where the department was much larger, many Jewish physicians, selected from the transports, helped Dr. Mengele. Usually those who helped were assigned a room in the family section of Birkenau and were allowed to bring the other members of their family to live with them.

At block 10 in the main camp, at the so-called Experimental Institute of Hygeine, the experiments performed were basically related to pregnancy. Young women were naturally or artificially fertilized, then were injected with various chemicals and the doctors observed the reactions. The physicians experimented with prolonging pregnancy and accelerating the delivery. They injected chemicals into the bloodstream to see what effect a given chemical would have on the development of a fetus. The babies born under such circumstances were immediately taken from the mothers for vivisection and eventual cremation.

Another experiment performed here involved freezing a man by having him sit naked in the freezing cold. Sometimes the process was accelerated by throwing water on him until he was almost dead. Then he would be put into a room with two naked young women. They were ordered to perform all kinds of sexual acts on him, and the physicians observed what effect all this had on the man's body. This experimentation probably was meant for the German army, because there were many cases of freezing among the soldiers fighting on the Russian front. There was a theory that a frozen person could be revived if a naked girl played sexually with him.

In Poland before World War II rabbits were used for such medical experimentation, so the unfortunate prisoners used for the experiments at this time were called "rabbits" and Block 10 was referred to as a "rabbit hutch."

The Jewish girls in Block 10 did not have to work. They had to report at least once or twice a day for medical checkups and experimentation, and received comparatively good food. They submitted quietly to their unhappy lot and submitted to whatever they were forced to do.

Dr. Mengele himself, who came to Block 10 from time to time, was especially interested in finding out how and why twins come into existence. Under his supervision, there was in Birkenau a special section presided over by a Hungarian Jewish doctor where, when twins were brought to Birkenau, they were killed and subjected to extremely detailed dissection and data collection. This was to reveal how the bodies of twins are alike and how they are different. In the main camp where the experiments were performed on pregnant women, he tried to find out the secret of the beginning of twins. This research was necessary because one of the leaders of German Hitlerism thought that it would be good to build the German population by helping German women artificially to produce twins instead of just one baby at a time.

A different kind of experiment was performed under Mengele's supervision in Birkenau. Here, for instance, the influence of temperature on the human body was studied. A prisoner would be undressed and submitted to extremely high temperatures. Data would be collected about the reactions of his body from the time he was exposed to the heat until the time he died. Next, experiments were made regarding all kinds of revival—cold water, chemicals, and so on. During the winter the same thing was done in relation to the extremely cold temperatures. A naked prisoner would be put outside in the bitter cold and his body would be carefully checked and data would be taken about heart function, body temperature, and so on, until he died.

Another experiment was with the effects of salt water on the body. A prisoner would be given only very salty herring to eat and, after two or three days, he would be given nothing further to eat or drink except salt water brought from the ocean for a period of two weeks. Again, all medical data were taken carefully and recorded in relation to the reaction of the heart, lungs, stomach, brain, and so on. The victim was used as long as necessary and then was sent to the crematorium.

Yet another kind of experiment was with simplifying emergency surgical operations. It was probably needed for cases on the front when it became necessary to operate on soldiers under battlefield conditions. Here an artifical emergency would be created—a prisoner would be shot, his hand or leg broken or cut off, and then all kinds of operations and healing processes would be applied in order to find the simplest and most successful method of taking care of the injury. Of course, as a result, the victim would be sent to the crematorium.

The German physicians and medical institutions were very interested in using the prisoners for all other kinds of research because, under normal circumstances, rabbits, mice, or monkeys were used and it was uncertain if the human body would react in the same way. Here they had an opportunity to check everything immediately on the body of a living human. So it was that often the experimental institutes in Auschwitz and Birkenau were visited by specialists in all fields of medicine from the universities in Berlin and other cities. Basically, these experiements were performed and data collected by the Jewish physicians, prisoners who, before their arrest, were practicing in hospitals in Germany, France, Hungary, and other countries of Europe occupied by Germany.

Prisoners young and old, male and female, were also

submitted to experiments with all kinds of epidemics and diseases—diptheria, malaria, and so on, and all kinds of suggested medications were given them.

The famous medical institution called by the Germans *Institut fur Rassenbiologische und Anthropologische Forschung* was interested in collecting all kinds of data concerning anthropology. Here was an opportunity for that because members of all segments of the European population were brought here. Therefore, before the corpses were sent to the crematoria, some were selected for this branch of the Institute where the Jewish doctors collected the data. After the data desired were collected, the body was sent to the crematorium. The name of the Institute I remembered because the experience I am about to relate imprinted the name on my mind forever. It took place while I was working in the disinfection section of the *effektenkammer*.

Near the *effektenkammer* in the same building, there was a photographic section. There the pictures of new prisoners were taken, but also photographic specialists worked here for the SS administration and for the Institutes of Medical Experiments.

One day an SS guard came to our room with a leather bag. He said that he had just come from the photographic department and wanted us to take care of the bag because he had some business in the kitchen. He told us that he would be back soon for the bag. We understood that he wanted to "organize" something in the kitchen.

When he left the room, the prisoner working with me suggested that we see what was in the bag. It looked as if he had already "organized" something, for when we opened the bag we saw something packed in paper with blood on the top of the paper. My friend was sure that it was a nice piece of meat and he said that we should cut off a slice for ourselves. I readily accepted his suggestion. He locked the door and checked the window so that we would not be surprised by the guard, and I removed the paper. I was shocked to find in it the fresh head of a young girl. I called my friend and showed it to him. He, too, was shocked and we quickly repacked it and put it in the bag. On the top of the package was the name of the Institute for Anthropology.

Later I reported my experience to a friend, a young physician who was working in the hospital as a prisoner, and he told me that Dr. Mengele mentioned to him once that he was surprised that there were so many young Ukrainian men and women who looked more Germanic than some of the leaders of the Reich. Probably he had in mind Hitler, Himmler, and Goebbels, who, anthropologically, were anything but Germanic. This was probably the reason, my friend explained, that he selected especially Germanic-looking Ukrainian prisoners for collecting his data. When he met a blonde blue-eyed Ukrainian girl in the camp he simply ordered her shot and her head cut off so that the necessary pictures and measurements could be made of the structure of her skull.

Chapter 15

CHANGING REGIME IN AUSCHWITZ

At the end of 1943 and the beginning of 1944, big changes were made in the regime, the terror was loosened, and many other innovations took place in Auschwitz.

The *kommandant* of Auschwitz, SS Lieutenant Colonel Rudolf Franz Hess, a known sadist, was replaced by Libbehenschel, a much more humane *kommandant* than his predecessor. In his statement during his trial after the war, Hess said that he was released from duty as *kommandant* of Auschwitz on December 1, 1943.

After Hess was replaced, one day in December the *kapos* and *blockältesters* had a roll call and were told by the new *kommandant* that they would no longer be permitted to torture the prisoners. The regime continued to be harsh, but no special torturing of prisoners was allowed. The *kapos* and *blockältesters* thought this new order was a joke, but they soon found out that the *Kommandant* was serious.

One day he witnessed a bestial torturing of a prisoner by a *kapo*. The *Kommandant* ordered the *kapo* to put his prisoner number on paper, and after roll call he was officially given twenty-five lashes for this senseless torturing. This punishment of a *kapo* was unheard of, and the prisoners began to have hope that perhaps life might be a little easier on them under the new *kommandant*.

Most important to our survival, though, was that the

selecting and helping of prisoners to die in the *krankenhaus* was controlled by order of the *kommandant*. I have mentioned before that at least once a week there was an inspection in the hospital by a German doctor assisted by an SS. At this time, the very weak or incurably ill prisoners were sent to Birkenau to be gassed. At other times, sick prisoners were given a poisonous injection to help them die. Now this was limited.

During the trial of former SS guards Mulka and others, in December, 1963 in Germany, it was revealed that as a result of this practice of "helping" prisoners die, in the period between the summer of 1943 and the end of 1944, some 130,000 prisoners in KL Au 1 were "helped" to die.

Now that this was controlled, the prisoners had some hope that when they got sick they would be treated in the hospital rather than being almost without exception candidates for the poisonous injections.

At the end of 1944 a new, heretofore-unbelievable unit was formed called the *blockschonung*. This meant that a prisoner who was sick seriously enough to be unable to work but not enough to be sent to the hospital was permitted to remain in this room even during the roll call.

Roll calls were reduced at this time also. The morning roll call was dropped and only the night roll call was carried out as before.

The procedures surrounding the execution of prisoners were changed, too. Prisoners caught stealing, instead of being executed, were given twenty-five lashes. The hangings which we had witnessed quite frequently after night roll call were now quite rare. Also, the left wing, the practice of selecting prisoners for execution and taking them to Block 11, was now either dropped entirely or drastically reduced.

After the war, Colonel Hess gave an interesting statistical report about what happened in the camp during the time he was *kommandant* of KL Au. He said that he commanded Auschwitz until December 1, 1943. He estimated at least 2.5 million Jewish prisoners were exterminated by gassing and/or burning. At least another one-half million, mostly non-Jewish, succumbed to starvation and disease, making a total dead of about three million. This additional one-half million dead represents from 70 to 80 percent of all persons sent to Auschwitz as prisoners and individually registered and not sent immediately to the gas chambers. These were those used as slave labor in the concentration camp industries. Included among the executed and burned were approximately twenty thousand Russian prisoners of war previously screened out of prisoner-of-war cages by the Gestapo. They were delivered to Auschwitz in Wermacht transports operated by regular Wermacht officers and men. The Jewish victims included about two million from Poland, 100,000 German Jews, and a great number of Jewish citizens of Holland, France, Belgium, Hungary, Czechoslovakia, Greece, and other countries. The non-Jewish victims, called "Aryan," represented all countries in Europe occupied by Germany.

The loosening of the system of terror in Auschwitz made all the prisoners relatively more comfortable. Replacing the hangings for stealing with twenty-five lashes encouraged the growth of stealing. Everyone who had a chance tried to steal something to eat or something which could be exchanged for good. Even the SS began to cooperate with the prisoners in this respect.

Another important change brought about by the new *kommandant* was that the prisoners began to be paid for their work. At the end of each week, each prisoner received a coupon worth one mark. For this one mark he could buy a pack of cigarettes or a vegetable sausage—a sausage filled with vegetables instead of meat—or even soup. This was especially beneficial to the smokers who heretofore had had to exchange some of their food for cigarettes.

I found out what smoking means to a smoker in an experience with a good friend. Once a month we were taken to the washroom to take a shower. During the winter, as well as the summer, we were undressed to our wooden shoes and had to run to Block 1 where, in a wooden barracks between Blocks 1 and 2, there was a big washroom. After taking our shower, we returned to our block. An SS accompanied us from our block and back after we had finished our showers.

One night when we came back wet and naked, the SS with us began to smoke, but when his duty was finished he dropped the cigarette on the floor and left. A friend of mine, a hard smoker, grabbed the cigarette and began to smoke it. Since it was forbidden to smoke in the room on the penalty of ten to twenty-five lashes, he decided to finish the cigarette outside. The temperature was about zero degrees, but by jumping around and performing all kinds of gymnastics, he was able to remain outside long enough to finish the cigarette. Later we teased him about a love for a cigarette so strong that it made him unaware of the extreme cold. But now, due to the new regulations regarding pay, all smokers had the opportunity to buy a package of cigarettes each week.

Also at this time prominent prisoners were permitted to have linen on their beds and good blankets. They were also permitted to have socks and pullovers. Officially no one was given any of these, but the relaxing of rules made it possible for the prisoners working in the laundry and the *effektenkammer* to steal these articles and smuggle them out to be sold to the other prisoners.

On Sunday the prisoners were allowed to organize soccer teams and play soccer and other sports. Of course, only the *kapos*, *blockältesters*, and some of the prominent prisoners were able to take advantage of the opportunity, but it was, nevertheless, a change for the better.

In the middle of 1944 a brothel was even organized. About twenty strong young girls from among the prisoners were selected and placed in Blocks 10 and 22A. Each of these girls had to serve six customers per night. It was puzzling to me then and still baffles me as to the kind of limitation set on the customers. The prisoners from eastern Europe were not permitted to use the brothel, only the prisoners from central and western Europe. Coupons were distributed to each *kapo*, and the *kapos* gave coupons to the best working prisoners. In this case, I had the chance to take advantage of being registered as a Czech, but, when I was given a coupon one day, I told the *kapo* I was really a Ukrainian and therefore not permitted to go to the brothel.

Up to this time prisoners who became mentally ill from the horrors they were subjected to had been taken to the hospital and given a poisonous injection. Now, this was no longer permitted. A part of the *krankenhaus* was set aside for these prisoners where they were given some treatment. They were not allowed to go out, but they could stand at the window and talk to the other prisoners.

I went there many times to see a Ukrainian boy about

twelve years old who had been sent to Germany as a slave to work for a German farmer. The boy had struck a cow that had stepped on his foot. For "striking a German cow," the boy had been arrested and sent to Auschwitz. When he took his place in the line for his first roll call here, the people standing next to him happened to be Slavic and spoke either Polish, Russian, or Ukrainian. They were talking about the crematoria because there was a breeze blowing the smell of the burning toward the prisoners standing for roll call. The boy asked what a crematorium was, and one of the prisoners, not knowing that it was the boy's first day, jokingly told him that it was where everyone eventually was sent and set on fire. When only the ashes remained, the prisoners told him, they were collected and sent to the family. It was too much for the young boy to bear, and he had to be sent to the *krankenhaus*.

One time after roll call, I was passing the *krankenhaus* and saw him standing at the window. He spoke especially beautiful literary Ukrainian and would often stand at the window and cry about the Ukraine, his mother and father and sister who were waiting for him, and the terrible fire that would burn them all. It was very moving to listen to him. I brought him what food I could and, in that way, tried to divert his attention from his misery.

The wires around the camp on the wall were electrified now only at night. Until this time at least ten prisoners each day would run to the wires and be killed by the electricity or be shot by the guards. It was preferable to some to commit suicide rather than continue living in the concentration camp. After the change in regulations in 1944, very seldom did a prisoner decide to commit suicide. Even if one had run into the wires, there was no electricity and the guards usually would only try to repel the prisoner by throwing stones at him.

In spite of all these changes completed first at the end of 1944, Auschwitz remained far from being a simple work camp. The extremely hard work continued, and although not as severe as before, the beatings of the prisoners also went on. In some cases the *kapos* and *forarbeiters* still "helped" prisoners to die. Many of the new prisoners had to go through a period of being *musulmen,* many still died of starvation, and the hangings continued, although not as often as before.

One hanging which remained imprinted on the minds of everyone took place in 1944. The man who was hanged was a former commissioned officer in the French army, a Jew. He was very strong physically and when he was brought to Auschwitz he tried to take advantage of working outside the camp by attempting an escape. He was caught and after night roll call was brought to the gallows to be hanged.

I had by then witnessed many such executions, but when the rope was placed around his neck, I closed my eyes for a moment to avoid seeing when he jumped from the platform. When I opened my eyes, I was very surprised. The prisoner was no longer there. The rope had broken and he had fallen. He slowly stood up and looked around, wondering where he was and what was going on. There was a great deal of confusion among the SS guards. They didn't seem to know what to do. The prisoners began to murmur that German criminal custom demanded that if a person is being hanged and the rope breaks, he should be given his freedom. After a few minutes of discussion among the SS, the prisoner was taken to Block 11 and shot. This was a clear demonstration to the prisoners that the Nazis obeyed no laws, not even their own.

Chapter 16

HUNGARIAN JEWS

The practice of bringing Jews from all over Europe into the camp to be gassed continued. Now came the time for the Hungarian Jews to be brought. Until 1944 Hungary was regarded as an independent state. There was no unit of the Gestapo there and the Germans did not interfere in the internal workings of the country. In 1944 the Germans suggested that since the Russian army was nearing Hungary from the east, it would be beneficial for the Hungarians to destroy their Jewish population since "it is known that all Jews are sympathetic to Communism." This, the Germans asserted, was dangerous to the security of the Hungarian state. It would be good for all Hungarian Jews to be transported to Germany to work in the military industries. In that way the Hungarian state would be secure from danger within and the German industries would be aided at the same time. The Hungarian government accepted these arguments and so, in 1944, about four hundred thousand Jews from Hungary were transported to Auschwitz and gassed.

Everything was done in exactly the same way it had been with other transports of Jewish prisoners. A small group was selected to be sent to the main camp and the remainder were sent immediately to be annihilated in the gas chambers. Of the prisoners who were selected to remain with the regular prisoners, a new list was made starting with the number one, preceded by A and later by B. According to the registration, from the 400,000 Hungarian Jews brought to Auschwitz, about 20,000 were real prisoners and 380,000 were immediately gassed.

In 1944 our Ukrainian group was located in Block 17, just in front of the kitchen. Since the regulations were different now, and prisoners were not punished for having them, we smuggled linens from the laundry and *effektenkammer* for our beds. We also arranged it so that only two prisoners slept in each bed. Since we remained in the same room for a long time, our room was clean and relatively bearable.

One day in September, 1944 we were told not to go to work, but to remain in our room and gather up everything we had as we would be moved to another block. We wondered if we were going to be transferred to another camp, but a *blockältester* explained to us that we would be moved for only one day then brought back to the same room. We did not understand why.

From my position in the laundry, I could observe what was going on. A group of Jewish prisoners was brought and put not only in our room, but also in all the rooms of the block. We in the laundry were ordered to bring washed and ironed linens to the block and make nice beds with blankets from the *effektenkammer*. From the storehouses good civilian clothing was brought to the Jewish prisoners. Their camp dress was taken to the storehouses.

About noon, when soup was distributed to the prisoners, instead of the regular soup being given to them, barrels of the good soup prepared for the SS were brought to Block 17. It was puzzling, all these activities, but the puzzle was soon solved.

A delegation came to visit the camp. We were later told that the delegation included officials of the Hungarian government, the International Red Cross, an American Jewish organization, and others. They wanted to see if it was true that Hungarian Jews were brought not to a concentration camp but to a regular work camp. Therefore it was artificially arranged to make it look like Auschwitz was not a concentration camp at all, but a mere work camp.

During the day all prisoners were working outside the

camp, so the delegation couldn't see real prisoners. When the delegation was brought to Block 17, they saw prisoners dressed nicely, sitting on clean, well-made beds. They were allowed to test the soup and found that it was good. They were also permitted to talk to the prisoners. The prisoners had been advised to say only what the Gestapo told them to say. So when they were asked questions by members of the delegation, they said that this was really a good work camp, they lived together—the married in one place, the unmarried in another—they were permitted to have civilian clothing, they had good food and as much of it as they wanted, they were allowed to send letters as often as they liked, and so on. In general, they presented an extremely nice picture of the conditions. The delegation left the concentration camp with the impression that everything was just as German propaganda had said it was.

Immediately after the delegation left, the Jewish prisoners were ordered back into their prisoner garments and were transferred back to Birkenau and its harshness.

Among these Hungarian Jews were some who had lived in the Carpatho-Ukraine (called then also Subcarpathian Ruthenia) when it was occupied by Hungary, and therefore spoke Ukrainian. I found among them a high school professor and asked him why he didn't seize this opportunity to tell the delegation the truth about Auschwitz. He told me that if he had tried he would have been tortured, and all for no purpose. He said that the delegation was only seeing what it wanted to see, that if they did not believe that all Jews were brought here to be annihilated, how could they believe that everything they had been seeing was a farce? The concentration camp had paralyzed his normal powers of thinking and he was unable, in his mind, to explain to people who had never been in a place like this the horrors of a concentration camp. This was true of most of the prisoners.

It is also psychologically interesting to note that even in 1944, the Hungarian Jews didn't resist the German program for the annihilation. It was well-known of the two million Polish Jews delivered to the concentration camps only a few remained. The conclusion had to be that the remainder had been annihilated. When Jews were brought to Auschwitz from

Hungary, the inescapable conclusion was that they, too, would be annihilated. Yet when the Jews were ordered to report for their transports to Germany, they did not resist, but obeyed the orders. When they arrived at Auschwitz and were sent to the gas chambers, they didn't resist this, either.

As far as I know from the talk that passed around while I was at Auschwitz, there were only two cases of serious resistance. One group refused to leave the car at Birkenau. They knew where they were destined to go and tried to remain where they were. Of course, the car was open, so a detachment of SS was brought and the guards machine-gunned the people inside the car.

The other case of resistance was much more spectacular. In the fall of 1944 a *sonderkommando* of selected Hungarian prisoners barred themselves inside their block when it came their turn to be gassed. They had with them weapons they had organized in advance. A group of SS was brought there and a battle followed. As a result, all of the members of the *sonderkommando* were shot, or after some had surrendered, were thrown on the piles to burn. However, a number of the SS guards were also killed in the fighting. This was an exceptional case which proved that resistance could be performed. Psychologically, however, people were unable for the most part to take on this active resistance.

Another interesting case of resistance, occuring much earlier than these two by Hungarian Jews, was demonstrated by a Greek Jewish girl. She was a dancer and physically fit. When she was ordered to undress she realized what was going on. On the way to the gas chamber, she jumped an SS and took his knife. She killed him with it and cut another SS across the face. She was machine-gunned, of course, but she had managed to kill one SS and leave a document of resistance on the face of another for the rest of his life.

The prisoners were curious as to the far-reaching changes in the regime of the concentration camp. We were aware that these changes had been forced on the Gestapo. Voluntarily they would not have made the changes. One explanation was that many German soldiers had been taken prisoners by the English and American armies. The army headquarters, so the explanation went, had told the Germans that these prisoners would be subjected to the same kind of treatment given to prisoners in the German concentration camp. The changes were made, then, according to this theory, to give the impression that the Germans had accepted the English-American ultimatum.

Another explanation advanced was that the Germans had begun to realize that they were losing the war and were afraid for their own lives and their responsibility for the things they had done.

The man working with me, a member of the leadership of the Dutch Communist Party, told me that the Germans, at the end of 1943, began to realize that their armies were retreating into Germany at an alarming pace. They were afraid that they would be caught in the center of Germany with no place to escape and then all Nazis there would be put on trial. Perhaps Karl was right, but the most pleasing part of the explanation was that he had trusted me enough to repeat it to me. He was risking his life to say these things, because the *Politische Abteilung* would have executed him if his views had become known.

In the second part of 1944 another execution took place which was interesting in a different way. Ten prisoners were hanged for trying to escape by taking advantage of their positions in the canteen serving the SS. During a party they had given a great deal of whiskey to the officers, and while the drunken officers slept, the prisoners changed clothes with them. In a car of one of the SS they managed to get out of the camp. Two of them pretended to be Gestapo officers taking the other eight to Birkenau. Their escape was successful, but they were caught a few weeks later in Warsaw. They were brought back here and executed. For the first time during an execution, the prisoners shouted anti-German, pro-Communist slogans. This revealed that they had not been tortured before the execution as had previously been the rule. Other prisoners had been so tortured that they had been unable to shout anything. Even in the executions there were changes.

Chapter 17

IN THE SCHLACHTHAUSKOMMANDO

One day Karl told me that he had some good news. One of his friends who worked in the butchery had told him that the man who had been bookkeeper had been put on the list of those to be transferred to another camp, so they needed a new bookkeeper. Since Jewish prisoners could not work in the butchery, Karl had suggested me. The next day I was to report to the *kapo* of the *schlachthauskommando* and tell him that I had been sent by Karl.

I was very happy because working in the butchery was the dream of the prisoners. The butchery prepared all kinds of meat, not only for the prisoners but for the SS guards and members of the Air Force as well. There was, therefore, much opportunity to "organize" meat. I already knew that the meat used in the prisoners, soup was horse meat brought from the battlefield. For the SS and other members of the administration and the Air Force, hogs and cattle were killed and sausages were made.

The next morning I went to the *schlachthauskommando*, reported to the *kapo*, and repeated Karl's greeting to him. He ordered me to take the place of the transferred bookkeeper. My job was to make a record of everything brought to the butchery and how it was used. I found that the bookkeeping was in very bad order. There were many written reports from various people listing cattle and hogs and horses brought in, but there was no regular, day-by-day or account-by-account listing. So, before I began my bookkeeping, I had to put the previous accounts in order.

I wondered, even then, how it happened that I was allowed to work in the butchery so easily. Of course, it was partially because of Karl's connection with the *kapo*, who was also a member of the German Communist organization. Nonetheless, the Polish prisoners had a great deal of influence here, and I had expected that they would try to secure the position for a Polish prominent. I soon found out why even those who could have placed a Polish prisoner in this position preferred to let me have it.

The camp officials were expecting an inspection by the head office of concentration camps in Berlin. The situation in the butchery was so advantageous for stealing that everyone tried to steal whatever he could. Prisoners, SS, and even those sent from the SS kitchens to bring food tried to steal something. As a result, it was almost impossible to order the records so that this would not be discovered. Such a large quantity of meat was disappearing that the camp administration feared it would be discovered by the inspection team. The bookkeeper would be made responsible for the loss, arrested, taken to Block 11, and quickly executed. Thus, the case would be closed. So, in addition to having a good opportunity to "organize," I faced the prospect of being held responsible for the disorder in the bookkeeping.

After thinking about the situation for a few days, I found a way around my problem. I was told that when hogs were delivered for butchery 20 percent of their weight was to be subtracted to account for bones. The bones, however, were not thrown away but were powdered and delivered to chicken farms. So, from all the pieces of paper from the previous year listing the weights of meat delivered, I entered the amounts on them and then subtracted 20 percent. And after that, the same 20 percent I wrote off as delivered to the chicken farms. Of course, I realized that had my juggling of the figures been discovered by the specialists from Berlin, I would have been held responsible for the loss of meat, which would have meant my immediate execution. Nonetheless, this was the only thing available for me to try. Fortunately, the method was successful. The investigating team performed their inspection in a hurry and when they were told that there were one thousand pounds of meat in storage, they did not check to see if there really were that much meat, but only looked at my books to see if the figures were the same. They were pleased that all figures were correct. An inspector checked all my addition and subtraction and reported that the books were correctly kept. He was pleased to see that such careful records had been kept. The delegation left after visiting "Canada," where they tried to "organize" gold or something else of value left there by Jewish prisoners.

Of course, the *arbeitsführer* and *kapo* wondered how I had managed to cover up the loss of meat. They had been sure that the shortages and widespread stealing would be discovered.

The prisoners who managed to steal some sausage or bread during the day hid it somewhere until time to go back to the main camp. Then they would take what they had organized out of its hiding place and conceal it on their bodies somewhere, usually on their legs or stomach under the pants and coat. Since all the prisoners were skinny, it was not difficult to conceal something in this way. It was dangerous, however, because the prisoners in this *kommando* were searched quite often. A special opportunity presented itself whenever the *kommando* had worked past the normal time. Then when we returned to camp all the other prisoners were already standing in lines for the roll call, so we were not searched because the administration wanted to finish the roll call as soon as possible.

One day we had worked long enough to expect the guards to forget about searching us, so everyone concealed sausages on their legs, happy that there was no danger of discovery. When we passed the main gate, however, our group was halted and turned to the right. There the SS searched us. It was amazing to realize that the SS did not notice, or pretended not to notice, that when we performed our turn and two steps forward at his command that a sausage fell to the ground from the pants of every prisoner. When we moved the two steps forward, the sausages were then behind us. Row by row the *kommando* was searched and nothing was found on the prisoners.

Three prisoners who were working in the kitchen saw

what was going on and, without any order, walked behind us and gathered up the sausages. No one asked them who had told them to pick up the sausages or where they were being taken. The sausages were taken to their rooms as quietly as they had been picked up.

The SS guards working in the butchery did as much stealing as the prisoners. The guards did not like to be seen organizing by the prisoners, so they usually came into the butchery with their leather bags and pretended that they had some important document to deliver. Then, when they left, they simply placed a sausage or portion of meat in the bag.

In the butchery there was a veterinarian whose duty it was to check each piece of meat of the cows and hogs brought in to determine if it were fit for eating. If the meat were contaminated, it had to be refused. The veterinarian had a doctor's degree and was, therefore, a commissioned officer, not a real SS.

Among the SS on duty at the butchery was one called by the prisoners and other guards "the dirty dog." He was especially diligent in searching the prisoners and guards and suspected everyone of trying to take something out of the butchery.

One night when the veterinarian had finished his duties and was leaving, he was stopped by this guard and ordered to open his leather bag where his instruments were kept. He opened the bag and a big, long sausage was found in it. This "dirty dog" guard took the sausage out and, in the presence of the watching prisoners, struck the doctor on both sides of his face. This was an extremely unusual thing for a simple private to do—to strike a commissioned officer—and would ordinarily not have been overlooked. However, since the veterinarian knew he was guilty of stealing he did not react at all, but quietly came to attention. When the guard launched into a tirade and called him all kinds of evil names, the doctor simply answered, "Yes, sir. Yes, sir."

My duties as bookkeeper were to check all orders, enter the orders in the book, and make sure everything was correctly weighed for delivery in and out. When a cow or hog was delivered, I had to check its number and see if it corresponded to the number on the order accompanying it. Along with the number on the order was the weight of the cow or hog. Since I did this every day, I began to play a game of guessing the weights of the animals. One day an order came which said that the cow in question weighed 500 kilograms. The cow, however, was extremely small and skinny and it was impossible for it to weigh nearly that much. I checked the number once again, but there was no mistake. Then I weighed the cow and found that it weighed only 250 kilograms. Just to pass the time, I asked the veterinarian to join me in my guessing game. He said that the cow I had just weighed could not be heavier than 300 kilograms. I told him that he was in error and showed him the delivery report. He looked at the report, then at the cow and smiled. He told me that this was not unusual, then explained what had happened. He said that the SS responsible for bringing the cow from the farmer to the butchery had, instead, taken it to his home and substituted another, extremely thin, cow. Instead of delivering the cow weighing 500 kilograms, he had brought one weighing 250 kilograms. In that way he had managed to organize 250 kilograms of meat. It seems that the German supermen, the SS—officers as well as enlisted men—were accomplished thieves and took every opportunity to steal. They were no better than the criminals in the prisons and concentrations camps.

In the butchery *kommando* I met a French political prisoner who had been brought to Auschwitz at the same time as I. He told me that of the twenty-five hundred prisoners transferred from Paris to Auschwitz in July, 1942, only forty were still alive in this second half of 1944. All the others had died, most of them during the first three weeks of imprisonment.

After the fear of discovery by the team of specialists from the headquarters of the Administration of Concentration Camps in Berlin was over, I faced the possibility that I would be removed from the *kommando*. The *schreiber* of the butchery was a German-Polish lawyer from Prussia, Romanowski. He was eager to put one of the Polish prisoners in this good position, and had an opportunity to do this since the *arbeitsführer* was of Polish descent also, from Silesia. He was ready to support his compatriot in this way.

One day as we were leaving the butchery to return to the

main camp, the *arbeitsführer*, Jan, called me back into the room and told me that it was dirty, that I was responsible for it, and had to clean it before I left. Then he hit me in the face. I tried to explain to him that this was not my job since there was another responsible for the cleaning; I only kept the books. He shouted, *"Maul halten!"* ("Shut up!") and hit my face again. I immediately started cleaning, but was afraid because I had just placed a nice portion of lard in a bag on my stomach. It was easy to walk, but very inconvenient to lean down and clean the floor. I was afraid that he would discover that I had stolen the lard and would punish me even further. Nevertheless, I was able to finish the cleaning without discovery and left the butchery. The *kommando* was waiting and the *kapo* asked me why I had been so long. I told him what had happened and said that *Schreiber* Romanowski and *Arbeitsführer* Jan would probably prefer that I not return to the work in the butchery. He said that he would discuss it with the employment department.

When I reported to the *kommando* the next morning, I asked the *kapo* if I still was to go to the bookkeeper's job at the butchery. He said, "Sure, of course." Then he told me that he did not know what position I had in the Communist Party, but that Franz, a German prisoner heading the employment department, had told him that I must stay in the *kommando*. He was positive that I was a leading member of the Communist Party.

When the *kommando* arrived at the butchery, the atmosphere had changed remarkably. Romanowski came to me and told me that he had told the *arbeitsführer* that I was an extremely good bookkeeper and he had agreed. I no longer need have any fear of being thrown out of the *kommando*.

The next day I met Karl, with whom I had worked in the laundry, and he told me that I, a member of the Ukrainian Nationalist Organization that was bitterly opposed to the Communists as well as the Nazis, had, on his initiative, the support of the Communists in the camp. Karl said that from our detailed discussions he knew a great deal about my political ideology. He said our slogans, "Freedom for Every Nation," "Freedom for Every Person," "Social Justice," and "Prosperity for All" were what, in his opinion, Communism really meant. He said also that Russians were chauvinists and imperialists, not true Communists, and only used the ideology to cover their real motives. Actually they were just like the Nazis, holding to the idea of the superiority of Russians and dreaming of the occupation of the whole world. It was for these reasons that Karl said he liked my organization even though we called ourselves Ukrainian Nationalists.

At the end of 1943 the Russian offensive was brought into Ukraine. As a result, the prison in the capital of the western Ukraine, Lvov, was closed. A large group of the prisoners were brought to Auschwitz, but since there was no room for all of them, some were transferred farther west to the concentration camps in Germany.

The group which remained in Auschwitz was varied. There were Ukrainians, Poles, Jews, political prisoners, and criminals as well. Since two of our group were working in the *Politische Abteilung*, it was not difficult for them to catch the names from the list of the Ukrainian political prisoners. So, even though they were housed in different blocks and attached to different *kommandos*, we had no trouble contacting all of them. There were about 150, so our group, which had consisted of about 50 until that time, jumped to about 200 prisoners.

From them we received a great deal of news—news about the situation in Ukraine and about things that had happened during the past three years while we had been imprisoned. The information was especially detailed because among the new prisoners was one of the leaders of the underground movement.

We heard about the unbelievable oppression in the territories occupied by Germany. Contingents of young boys and girls were formed to be sent to Germany as slave workers. Each village was given a quota to be met. The propaganda said that these young people were to be "volunteers." Since the young boys often tried to escape to the forests and join the various underground movements, the Germans had to resort to other methods to fill the quotas. When there was a movie or other performance in a town, they would surround the theater and arrest all young men, regardless of who they might be. These would be added to the transport.

In order to keep the population under control, the Germans instituted a reign of terror. The quota system was used for gathering supplies—bread, meat and so on—to be delivered to the German administration and army. When the quota was not filled, the mayor of the town or someone suspected of being a member of the resistance was arrested. Some were sent to the concentration camps. Others were executed.

From the old times it was traditional in Ukraine for the farmers to hold a fair once a week in the towns. The farmers would come to the town to sell their farm products and buy the goods they needed. In the middle of each town there was a marketplace. It was in these marketplaces during the fairs, when they were crowded with people, that the Germans performed their executions. At least once each month in each town in the western Ukraine a group of prisoners would be brought to the marketplace for execution. Gallows were erected in the middle of the marketplace and the prisoners were hanged. A strip of paper with the inscription "Bandit" would be placed over the prisoners. The bodies remained there at least a whole day. This was done as a warning to the others that the same thing would happen to them if they tried to resist German authority.

The demand for farm products was extremely high and the collections so severe that in many places there was acute hunger or starvation among the farmers. In addition to this official form of robbery of the farmers, all the German soldiers and police took what they wanted from the farmers without paying them. The words *maslo, yayka* (butter and eggs) every German knew even if these were the only Ukrainian words he knew. They would come to the farmers and demand *"Maslo, yayka,"* and take whatever they found regardless of the fact that often this was all the farmer and his family, even small children, had to eat.

Because of this exploitation and persecution, the underground movement came out into the open and began fighting. A Ukrainian Insurgent Army was organized and began to fight first in the northwestern part of the Ukraine, Volynia, then in the western part, the Carpathian Mountains, and then even farther to the east. Many bloody battles took place between the Insurgent Army and the Germans. General Lutze, the commander of the SA, among others, fell in battle against the Ukrainian Insurgent Army.

Many of the prisoners were freed during the fighting, but here again the Germans applied their policy of "collective responsibility." In two cases in Volynia when many members of the Gestapo fell in battle, they simply called the army detachment, surrounded the village, started the houses on fire and machine-gunned the inhabitants as they tried to escape the fire. All inhabitants of these villages, including the women and children, were thus annihilated, and the villages were totally destroyed.

Badly hit on the western and eastern fronts, the Germans began to realize that they were losing the war and their plans, so carefully laid, began to falter. On the one hand, the Gestapo tried to carry out the orders of an increasingly irrational Führer. Hitler had issued the policy of "bald land," the total destruction of territories which had to be surrendered to enemies of Germany. The population, under this policy, was to be entirely annihilated and all buildings were to be burned. Nothing but the "bald land" was to remain. On the other hand, the army tried to follow a different policy. They began to try to take advantage of the anti-Communist mood of the people of eastern Europe by spreading the rumor that when Germany was defeated, since the United States came into the war to help all countries be free and Russia intended to dominate at least Europe, war would break out between America and Russia. Therefore, so the Germans said, detachments of the native population ought to be organized to help the German army fight against the Russian Communists since Germany would soon become an ally of the United States in a war against Russia. When the Germans started a detachment in Ukraine, many of the people fell prey to this line of "reasoning" and joined the detachment. They thought that this would be the nucleus of a group including the French, British, and American Armies which would fight against the Russians. A military unit called the Galizien Division came into being. About twenty thousand Ukrainians volunteered for this service. Opinion was sharply divided among the Ukrainians. Members and sympathizers of the Ukrainian Underground Movement and Ukrainian Insurgent Army were against organizing such a unit, because they felt that cooperation with Nazi Germany should, under no circumstances, be permitted. But there were many who were afraid to join the Ukrainian Insurgent Army and fight hopelessly against both the Russians and Germans. They preferred to join this military organization and fight only against the Russians with the help of the Germans. They hoped after the defeat of Germany they would find support from the United States and England in the continuation of their fight against Russia.

This was the third year since we had been brought to Auschwitz and we had been almost totally cut off from the flow of information about what was happening in Ukraine. Although I had managed to make some connections with German and French political prisoners who could secretly listen to American, British, and French radio broadcasts, there was still no information about Ukraine. This was because Russia and Poland were allies of the United States, England, and France. The prevalent opinion among the Allies was that all Ukrainians were divided into two groups—a large group that dreamed about the glory of Russia and cooperated with the Russian army, waiting for the moment when Russia would again occupy the whole Ukraine, and a smaller group that dreamed about the glory of Poland and did what they could to help Poland. Both the Russians and the Poles said that any others were just a small group of Nazi collaborators. Any information to the contrary—news about Ukrainians fighting against all occupying forces—was suppressed by the Russians and Poles. Reality was ignored and the Ukrainians fighting against Nazi Germany were never mentioned.

On the other hand, in their propaganda, the Germans tried to picture Ukrainians as happy with the German occupation and voluntarily cooperating with Germany in every respect. Only a small group, according to the information they released, obeyed the orders of Moscow and tried to resist Germany. This small group, they intimated, was made up of Communists only.

Even the Americans and British preferred to ignore the situation in Ukraine although they were familiar with it and had good information about what was happening. This was because they needed all the Allies to cooperate in the fight against Germany, and preferred not to offend Russia and Poland. The Ukrainian problem was a touchy one, and one, in their opinion, that would best be ignored for the time being.

Once a month each prisoner was allowed to write a letter to the one person he had cleared with the administration. With this person only was he allowed to correspond, and even then all correspondence was strictly censored. The censor for each territory was a German born and educated in that territory. As a result, the censors were familiar with the languages and could not be deceived by double entendre. Had a prisoner tried to smuggle information out of the camp in that way, he would have been severely punished.

The letter written from the concentration camp was one page long, in the prescribed form, and had to begin with the phrase, "I am in good physical condition and I feel very well." Then a few more sentences were allowed and the signature. Therefore, actually, although we were allowed to write, it was impossible to receive information about the political situation outside the camp.

From the uncensored, firsthand information brought now by the new prisoners we deduced that the collapse of Nazi Germany was unavoidable. We knew, however, that Germany was still strong militarily and that it would take some time longer for the actual collapse to come.

One bit of bad news was brought by the new prisoners. They said that it was known that, according to the orders of the Nazi leadership, in case of the collapse of Germany, no prisoners other than Germans were to be permitted to survive. In the last moment, German prisoners were to be separated and freed and all others were to be annihilated. This was so that there would be no witnesses to tell the world what had happened in the Nazi concentration camps. This was not a cheerful prospect for us, but we knew this was only an opinion and so we did not give up hope that we would survive not only the concentration camp, but also this "final solution" as well.

Psychologically, the most important thing was we were already used to living under the threat of death. Death was around us every day, taking victims one by one and we had accustomed ourselves to the thought that we might very well be next. Therefore the information that everyone would have to die if Germany fell made less impression on us than an "F" on a report card makes on a high school student.

Taking advantage of the relaxation of regulations in the camp, we began once more as we had in Monelupich Prison to organize a semblance of a cultural life. After the work in the evening we met in our rooms and the poets and authors began to write again. The bachelors among us began a correspondence with some of the girls in Birkenau. Among the prisoners transferred from Lvov were about a dozen Ukrainian girls. They were put in Birkenau, but one of them belonged to the *kommando* that came to the kitchen in the main camp to take food to the female prisoners. One of our group who worked in the kitchen used his contact with her to smuggle our letters to the girls.

One day the prisoner working in the kitchen did not deliver the letter he had been given, but kept it until that evening. When we met together to report the news of the day and read to each other, he opened the letter and began to read it. It was written to a girl named Oksana. Listening to the letter, one and then another said, "I, too, am writing to her." We discovered that there were twelve writing to the same beauty. It was a humorous situation. One suggested that these twelve, instead of fighting, should organize themselves. Thus, Oksana Knights Order was brought into being. Some refused to join, so we formed an anti-feminist Old Bachelors' Order as well. These groups provided a great deal of amusement for us because we wrote anthems, poems, and so on expounding the virtues of the various points of view about Oksana and women in general.

A spectacular illustration of the changes of the regime in Auschwitz in 1944 was the wedding of a German political prisoner performed in Auschwitz. The prisoner was a member of the Communist International Brigade which had fought in Spain against Franco. There he had met a Spanish girl and they had two children. When he came back to Germany he tried to bring her with him. Before he was able to get her to Germany, he was arrested and placed in the concentration camp. Since he had not had an official wedding, his wife and children were refused support from the German authorities. Now the new *kommandant* gave permission for the wedding to take place in the concentration camp. So one day she came with the children to the main camp and an official performed the ceremony in the SS administration office. A room was set aside for the newlywed couple and they, along with the children, were taken to the room at the end of the camp while the orchestra played. This event was so unusual that the prisoners were forced to admit that there had been a real change in the administration.

This story, however, didn't have a happy ending. After the wedding, the wife and children were sent home and she began receiving support. A few months later her husband, along with some others, tried to escape. He was caught and was one of the few prisoners, as I have mentioned before, who was hanged during this time. Nevertheless, because of the humanity of the new *kommandant*, his wife and children were able to receive support from the German authorities and a legal ceremony had been arranged.

At the end of 1944 the new *kommandant* did something else very unusual. The political department of the Gestapo at Auschwitz, until this time, had engaged secret agents from among the prisoners. These agents spied on their fellow prisoners and reported what they had seen and heard to the *Politische Abteilung*. The new *kommandant* didn't like this practice, so when a demand came for prisoners to be sent to the stone quarry at another camp, he asked the *Politische Abteilung* to make a list of the secret collaborators. These men he put on the list to be sent to the quarry. This list became known to the other prisoners and, when all these collaborators were gathered into one room in preparation for their transport, some of the prisoners broke in and severely beat the spies.

The Polish prisoners took advantage of the new attitude of the new *kommandant*, and when a prison at Lodz was closed and all prisoners transported to Auschwitz, they took the opportunity to punish a Polish prisoner who had been an open collaborator with the Gestapo. He had worked as an undercover agent for a long time, then worked with the administration in beating and torturing prisoners until they admitted the things he had found out about them. At the same time, he pretended to be a prisoner. He was hated by all political prisoners in Lodz. Everyone who came from Lodz mentioned the horrible agent of the Gestapo, Sowa. Now, when with all the other prisoners, he was transferred to the concentration camp, the political prisoners who knew him came to the reception office to meet him. When Sowa started the reception procedure, the prisoners jumped him and severely beat him. He managed to run away and ran straight to the barbed wire, hoping to be killed with the electricity. There was no electricity in the fence during the day and the SS guard tried to force him away by throwing stones. He was afraid to come down because, not far from the wire, a crowd of prisoners was waiting to continue beating him. Finally the SS guard made use of his gun and Sowa was hit a few times. He didn't die immediately, but fell to the ground crying to his compatriots for pity. They beat him until he was dead. The guards didn't try to intervene. After he was dead and the Polish prisoners had left, one of the physicians came and took his body to the hospital. There was no investigation ordered by the administration.

The radical changes in the regime didn't come overnight. When they did come they were met with suspicion and distrust by the prisoners. When I became quite ill one day, I refused to go to the hospital, fearing that I still might get a poisonous injection. The sickness had come upon me quite unexpectedly. During the time I had been a *musulman* an epidemic took hundreds of people each day, many of whom had been sleeping in the same bed with me. I happened to be immune and survived that epidemic. Now, when I was working in the butchery and was a prominent, I didn't expect to become sick. One night when we returned from work and were passing the orchestra, one of the leaders of the administration didn't like our marching and ordered us to stop. The *kapo* received a reproof and was furious. Instead of allowing us to go to our blocks, he decided to use the hour remaining before the beginning of roll call for disciplinary exercises. We were taken to a space between the blocks, and for an hour had to run, fall down, get up, crawl on our knees and elbows, and then repeat the whole procedure. After an hour, no one was able to stand up. We were exhausted and since there were a few minutes yet remaining before roll, everyone tried to relax. It was fall and the snow had already started to fall. The ground was very wet, so I found a handcar and lay on the iron part of the car to relax off the wet ground. I didn't realize that because I was wet and it was so cold, lying with my back on the cold iron was extremely dangerous. After the roll call was over I already felt a little discomfort. In the morning my temperature was quite high. My friends told me to go to the hospital, but I was afraid and decided to go to work instead. Even with a high temperature I continued to work for another week and during that time defeated the sickness. I didn't realize at the time how ill I had been. After the liberation, when I underwent a physical examination by a German physician, he asked me when I had had an acute infection of my lungs and lung membranes. When I told him, he was amazed that I had survived. He said that it had been his experience that even with good care only one in a thousand survived such infections. He asked me who my physician had been; he said that he must have been an expert. I answered that I had had the best physician in the world—my will to survive.

Chapter 18

THE CONTINUED ANNIHILATION

But the mills of death continued to work. Although so many changes were brought to KL Au 1, the work of the gas chambers and the crematoria in KL Au 2 (Birkenau) continued.

At the end of 1943, annihilation of the entire Jewish population of Poland had been almost completed. From about 3.5 million Jewish Polish people who had lived in Poland when World War II began, 2.5 million lost their lives in the gas chambers and crematoria of Auschwitz; another 1 million died in ghettoes like Warsaw and in small camps like Treblinka.

At the beginning of 1944 the annihilation of the Jewish population of Hungary began. The same procedure was followed as had been used in Poland. Every day between five and ten thousand prisoners were transported to Auschwitz and went through the procedure of selection for those to become regular prisoners and those to be sent to the gas chambers. During this time about four hundred thousand Jews from Hungary were thus murdered.

In the summer of 1944 the Germans turned on the gypsies. In Birkenau a special section had been set aside for the occupation of gypsies who were also German citizens. Because of their citizenship they had been spared immediate liquidation. They had been living there a long time and therefore believed that they would not be sent to the gas chambers.

One day, however, they were ordered to prepare for transport to another camp. They received a double portion of bread and some other food, indicating that they would be in the transport for a long time before they would get to the new camp. Then they were taken to the shower room for disinfection. Instead of a shower, they were gassed. In one day a gypsy camp where about five thousand prisoners—men, women and children—had lived, ceased to exist.

At the beginning of the fall of 1944 the last group of Polish Jewish prisoners came in from ghettoes in Litzmanstadt (Lodz in Polish). About fifty thousand who remained there were liquidated.

At the end of 1944 transports of Czech Jews, who had been placed in a special camp at Teresienstadt until that time, began to come.

At the end of 1944 the time came for Camp C. This was a part of Birkenau where selected Jewish female prisoners had been housed. At one time there had been between ten and fifty thousand prisoners. From among them candidates for slave work in German industry had been selected. When there was a need for a labor force, representatives from the given industry came and selected those they needed. Those who were to weak for work were sent to the gas chambers. At this time there were about twenty thousand prisoners in Camp C. They were all sent to the gas chambers.

Therefore, all gas chambers, piles, and crematoria continued to work in the same way they had before. The new, more humane, *kommandant* added to the 2.5 million prisoners liquidated by Hess, about another one-half million.

All this was known to the prisoners in the main camp because a small group cut off from the main transports was sent to the main camp every day. They reported to the other prisoners where they were from and how many others had come with them. Knowing all this, we were afraid that once the step-by-step liquidation of Birkenau had been completed, all non-German prisoners in the main camp would be next in line. The situation was very confusing because, on the one hand there were the many changes in the regime which I have detailed, but on the other hand, there was the continuation of the liquidation of not only Jewish prisoners, but also non-Jewish prisoners such as the gypsies and *mischlings*, the half-Jewish prisoners. Among these were some who had one German parent. When even these were sent to the gas chambers, we couldn't expect anything good to happen to us when Nazi Germany collapsed.

We couldn't understand why the Hungarian government was cooperating with the German government in sending all the Jews to Auschwitz. Although the Hungarian government had been told that all these people were being sent to labor camps, there was no longer any secret in Europe about what was happening in Auschwitz.

Once I met a Hungarian Jew who had been sent to the main camp. When I asked him what he thought about this, he put it this way: "It is true that the Hungarian government knows what is going on in Auschwitz. They know what is happening to the Jewish population there. When they began to send the Jews, they realized that if Hungary is occupied by Russia all Jewish people would take revenge for those sent to the gas chambers. They feared that for about one hundred thousand Jews sent to the gas chambers, the surviving Jews would take revenge in equal numbers on the Hungarian population. Therefore, they preferred not to permit even one Jew to survive. So the cooperation with the Gestapo in sending all others to the gas chambers continues."

At the end of 1944 the number of registered prisoners, excluding all those who had been immediately sent to the gas chambers, went over five hundred thousand male prisoners and four hundred thousand female prisoners. Now only about seventy thousand still survived. What would now happen to these at the end of the Third Reich?

Chapter 19

EVACUATION OF AUSCHWITZ

On January 12, 1945, the Russians began an offensive from a line south of Warsaw in a southwest direction with the aim of capturing all of Silesia. Auschwitz concentration camp was located in Silesia, therefore an evacuation of the camp began in the next few days. Even so, the official military reports continued to picture the situation as "controlled" and everything happening according to the plan as it was called *"planmassig."* It was no longer a secret that the retreat of the German army was chaotic and panicky.

The first group of prisoners was made up of Germans. They were separated out and transferred in cars to other concentration camps in the central German territory. The only Germans who remained were the *kapos* and *blockältesters* necessary to help in the evacuation of the others.

On January 17 the last regular roll call was held. Records concerning this roll call produced after the war in the war criminals trials state that there were present on this day in 1945 48,342 male prisoners and 16,096 female prisoners, a total of 64,438.

The prisoners were not evacuated all at the same time, but were divided into groups. The first evacuation began in Birkenau. On the seventeenth a large group of prisoners were placed in the section of the crematoria then were removed and the crematoria were dynamited and burned. The other parts of Birkenau followed. In the main camp the evacuation began on January 19. On the seventeenth we had seen the fire in Birkenau, heard the detonation, and were very confused because we didn't know what was taking place there. Many suspected that prisoners were not being evacuated at all, but were being dynamited in their blocks. Some suspected that the same thing would be done in Auschwitz. This suspicion was based on the fact that we had seen a group of SS in working clothes a few days before going around the camp checking all underground connections. The prisoners suspected that they were placing dynamite for the demolition of the whole camp.

But on January 19 we were ordered *"antreten"* and a big group of about two thousand was formed. It was made randomly. We had to be ready to march, then had to wait, then again form lines, then again sit down, so that the whole night we were running around but remaining in the camp.

Since the camp had to be abandoned and no one cared any longer about the storehouses, they were all opened on the seventeenth and the prisoners were allowed to take whatever they wanted. Expecting evacuation in the next hours, the prisoners came to the storehouses and tried to take as much meat, bread and other food as possible. Some even took watches and other precious things they happened to find.

In the morning of January 20, our group was finally formed and began to walk to another camp. Outside we met another group coming from Birkenau. They joined us and we walked northwest. After a few hours we were stopped because another group preceding us had been captured by the Soviet army. Therefore we had to go southwest.

The temperature was below zero degrees, but the administration had permitted the prisoners to wear regular clothing which had been marked with a red stripe on the front and back. This red stripe made it visible that one was a prisoner, but in the last days the prisoners had taken sweaters, pullovers, and such things so no one was really exposed to the cold. We marched in rows five by five guarded on both sides by SS with machine guns. For about ten prisoners there was one SS guard. Almost every prisoner had a rucksack filled with bread, meat, and other things. Even though we hadn't received regular food, everyone had had enough to eat. After a few hours of walking, however, the first prisoners began to fall. Then we discovered an especially cruel procedure. As a prisoner fell, he was shot in the head and pushed aside. At the end of the column there was a group of ten SS guards who checked all fallen prisoners to make sure they were dead. They crushed the skulls to be sure that no one survived. We at first did not understand the reason for this, but it soon became obvious that we would be followed by the advancing Russians, and the Germans didn't want any living witnesses to their cruelty. However, nothing would have been easier than for the Russians to take films documenting the brutality of the German nation.

A *transportführer*, the SS officer responsible for the transportation of the group, was evidently extremely nervous. So were his helpers. They rode on motorcycles at the front of the group, then to the rear, then again to the front, shouting and checking constantly. The march itself was chaotic. Very often we were ordered to push together and the SS made a circle around the group holding their guns, then everything would be changed back as it had been before the march continued. For a while the SS walked beside his ten prisoners, then it was changed to three SS walking together, watching a group of thirty. This was probably done to prevent a prisoner from attacking a lone guard and capturing his gun. A large number of prisoners were exhausted, perhaps because of all the running around done on January 19 and 20, preparing for the evacuation. The Ukrainian group was walking near the end of the column and we saw that about every one hundred feet there was a dead prisoner lying beside the road.

Our group had managed to stay together, and this was to our advantage already in the first hours of the march. Among us there were two who were sick and had no one to care for them. They would have been among the first victims with broken skulls had not the rest taken care of them by placing them on a handcart and taking turns pushing the handcart. After about two or three hours, one of the German prisoners, a *lageraltester* from Birkenau, saw that we had a handcart and threw the prisoners off the cart and put his rucksack on it. He told us to push it for him. Before he even finished his order, he was attacked from all sides. His rucksack was thrown down, our friends were put back on the handcart, and he was beaten. He jumped to the front of the column and called for help. The SS men came and asked him what was going on, then asked us what had happened. The SS knew us and told the German, "I can help you with these prisoners, but I can tell you that before I finish shooting them all, you would die first and then I would die next. These Ukrainians will die for one another, and so I suggest that it would be better for you to stay away from them." The German never came back to bother us.

A Jewish prisoner fell a little later and was shot in the head, but he jumped up and began to run. As he ran he cried, "They want to kill me, but I want to live and so I will survive." It was not possible for him to survive, however, because the wound was so severe. After running and shouting for another two or three minutes, he fell down again. Another guard shot him and his skull was crushed.

At night we stayed at farms selected by the SS in advance. We were placed in the stockyards, barns, and sheds among the cattle. All those who found a place under a roof were glad even when they had to sleep among pigs, cows, or calves, because it was cold outside.

After the first such night, Luks, who never lost his sense of humor, reported to us when we continued to march, "You know, I had a dream that I escaped, came home, and met my darling. She ran to me and started to kiss me very affectionately. As I pushed her away, I awakened. Then I found out I was pushing away a calf who was licking my face with its tongue." He told us that he would play a trick on the SS the next night. When we were put in among the cattle, he took a place not far from the door. Outside the door was an SS guard. After midnight, Luks took two calves, brought them to the door and kicked them, forcing them to jump out. The SS heard the opening of the door and wanted to see what was going on. The first calf jumping out hit him in the stomach with its head. He fell down, sure that he had been hit by escaping prisoners. He shouted an alarm, jumped up, and began to shoot. Lights were turned on and machine guns were put into operation. The terrified calves ran toward the gate and before it was discovered that they were not prisoners, they were machine-gunned. The next morning the prisoners were talking about an attack by partisans and the successful escape of a group of prisoners. We smiled because we knew what had happened to cause the alarm among the SS. As we were leaving the farm, we saw the two victims of the shooting being taken away by the farmer. Luks looked with sympathy at them and said, "I feel guilty. After the war I should be tried for cooperation with the Nazis for killing two innocent calves." He didn't survive the war, but died during the last days and couldn't be brought to trial for his "crime."

After two days of marching in zigzags to avoid the Russian army, we entered Czechoslovakia. Most prisoners had already eaten what they had in the rucksacks and the regular food was not delivered as it should have been. Prisoners began to be hungry and thirsty. Now we found out that the Czechoslovakian people were very sympathetic to us. They were warned in advance that it was forbidden to help the prisoners; the penalty for this would be shooting. Many, especially girls, disregarded the warning and waited for the prisoners. When we had to pass under a bridge, many threw pieces of bread and other food down to us. When we passed in front of houses in the village, young girls brought water on one side, left the cans on the road and ran to their houses. We were pleased with the food and water, but the sympathy we encountered was even more important.

I think that no one was punished for helping the prisoners because the SS guards were too busy keeping the prisoners from escaping. Also they were all thinking about what was to happen to them. They knew that the war would soon end and Nazi Germany would cease to exist. Then they all would have to answer for their crimes.

One day, when we were crossing a forest, our transport was attacked by partisans. All prisoners were ordered to fall to the ground and remain still. The SS began to return the fire with their machine guns. It seems that the partisans were weak, because about an hour later everything was over, and we were ordered to continue.

There was a small chance of escaping, but the risk was too great since there were so many SS with machine guns.

But, first of all, all prisoners believed there were only three or four weeks left before Germany would collapse.

After four days of marching, we came to a railroad station. There we were put in freight cars. After two days of traveling in the cars we stopped and were ordered to leave the train at a small station called Mauthausen.

Chapter 20

MAUTHAUSEN

The freight train transporting the prisoners made its last stop just outside the Austrain town of Linz. This was probably a special station for the Mauthausen concentration. Here all prisoners were ordered to leave the train. A column was organized and we walked toward the camp.

The concentration camp itself was located on the top of a hill among beautiful mountains. From the distance it looked like a medieval castle. The road between the rocks was new, and while we walked on it we saw prisoners working on building the road and in the stone quarries on either side of the road. Now I could see what would have happened to me had I been sent a year earlier to the stone quarry.

Soon we arrived at the concentration camp. Although the walls around the camp were stone, the buildings themselves were just wooden barracks. It was late afternoon and we were taken to a big wooden barracks where real showers were located in order to pass through the normal reception procedure—undress, take a shower, receive new camp dress, and be transferred to the blocks.

Between the barracks and the wall which surrounded the camp there was a backyard, narrow but very long, and all prisoners were put there. When it was time for the first group of prisoners to go to the shower, it was discovered that because of the low temperatures the pipes had frozen and burst, so we had to remain in that backyard until the showers were repaired. It was very cold, the prisoners were tired after a week of marching and riding, and everyone wanted to get through the procedure as soon as possible in order to' be able to relax a few hours at least in a warm room. Therefore, everyone fought to get to the front so that when the pipes were fixed they would be among the first to take a shower and be sent to the rooms. The fixing of the showers didn't happen, however, A group of prisoners tried to push their way through and the *kapos* and *blockältesters* tried to hold them back with clubs and iron bars. When the rest saw this, they were afraid and came back, but those in front, a dozen or so, fell to the ground and died.

After about thirty minutes, the same thing happened again. The group went a little too far, there was hitting and beating, one or two dozen fell down, and the others came back.

We were ordered then into ten long rows. On both sides of the rows of prisoners there was enough space to lie down and since many were exhausted, they decided to lie down and wait until their turn to go to the shower. Soon some fell asleep. But after a few hours, the rows were broken and the whole group tried to get in front again, expecting the showers to be working. When the beating began, the group retreated in panic, running over those lying in the snow. All those who had been lying down were trampled to death.

A little while later, the tiredest among us moved the dead to a place alongside the wall and took their places between the rows. They did not think the same thing would happen to them. However, the macabre rush to the front and panicky retreat over the bodies of sleeping prisoners continued the whole night. Many hundreds of incoming prisoners died during the night, and another wall of frozen corpses grew up.

Because the transport was very large, there was no time for shaving, so the prisoners had to only undress, take a shower, be smeared with disinfectants, and be carefully searched. I tried to take a picture with me of my family which I had received in my last letter. I asked the *kapo* to permit me to keep it since it would probably be the last thing I had from my parents and brothers and sisters in my life, but as an answer I got a kick in the face. He took the picture and threw it away.

When another prisoner was ordered to bend, the *kapo* discovered that he had tried to smuggle in a $100 bill in plastic on his abdomen. The bill was taken out and the naked prisoner got 25 lashes. While he was crying out from the punishment, a friend of mine who had tried to smuggle a little gold watch under his tongue became afraid that he would be discovered and swallowed the watch. After we finished the procedure and came out, he told us what had happened. We made fun of him and told him that although the watch might still be working, it would be very inconvenient for him to find out the time. Nonetheless, a day later he passed the watch, unharmed, and sold it to the *blockältester* for two pounds of bread.

I later found out that during the transportation and while waiting for the showers, more than one thousand prisoners died. The rest, about five thousand, were put into three barracks. The overcrowding was terrible. There were no beds, and we had to stand because there was no room for lying on the floor. This we had to do one whole day. We received food similar to that in Auschwitz at the proper time. At night we were ordered to take a special position for sleeping. There was no room for normal sleeping, so the administration had come up with a very original system. All prisoners were told to get into lines. The last line sat down and inclined their knees. The next line sat between the knees of the prisoners behind them and the other lines followed. In this way it was possible for all prisoners to sit on the floor. In this position we had to sleep with our heads on the shoulders of the prisoner in front or the chest of the prisoner behind.

The place where we were taken was known as Mauthausen concentration camp, but was administratively only the main body of the camp. It had many branches located in different places in Austria. Each branch had its own name according to the town it was located near. In this way people who were unfamiliar with the administration would think there was only one concentration camp, Mauthausen, when in fact there were many all over Austria.

Since the main camp was so badly overcrowded the administration began forming groups and sending them to other branches of the camp. Our group was divided, and my turn to go came on the third day. A group of about one thousand was formed and sent to the branch called Melk.

On those three days that we were in the main camp of Mauthausen, we were not sent to work, but remained in our barracks. We left the building only for the morning and evening roll calls. Many more prisoners died during this time. When one died during the night, no one bothered to take the body out of the room, so the prisoners had to hold the corpse of a friend on their chest or shoulders until morning. During the morning roll call the dead were taken out.

This camp had something new—the camp police—which didn't exist in Auschwitz. This was a group of German prisoners who were good-looking and well-dressed. They assisted in food distribution and keeping order in the camp. One of these prisoners proved to be friendly, and gave us a brief history of the camp. We found out from him that Mauthausen had been built in 1940 for former fighters against Franco who had been found by the Germans in France after the occupation by the German army. Ten thousand of these former soldiers of the Spanish Republican Army had been brought here and began the building of Mauthausen. From Dachau about five hundred strong, young German prisoners were brought to be the camp police. The idea was that since all these men were anarchists they needed to be taught by the Germans how to obey orders. That these police were good teachers we had seen when we were waiting for the showers and when we were escorted from the shower room to the barracks. The police hit and beat these prisoners with rubber clubs. Each member of the camp police carried a club or stick. In the rooms where we stayed, they made use of the clubs and sticks not only during the food distribution, but also when we had to change places for sleep. When one was a little slow in sitting down, he was struck in the head with a club so that he fell down. In this way the procedure was performed quickly.

With this policeman who seemed to be friendlier than the others, one of the prisoners who sat near me made a deal. He had taken a dozen gold watches from the storehouse at Auschwitz and had hidden them on his legs. When he came to

Mauthausen and were waiting in the yard for our shower, he managed to hide all the watches in the snow in the corner of the yard. He suggested to the policeman that he could sell him some nice watches. He took him out and promised to pay one loaf of bread for each watch. The prisoner recovered the plastic bag he had wrapped the watches in, concealed six of the watches on his legs, and sold the other six to the camp policeman. This was very unusual, because the camp policeman could have simply taken the watches rather than pay the prisoner for them. In this, too, he proved to be more honest because he actually gave the prisoner the bread he had promised him.

On the third day as we were being put into lines to go to the new camp, the policeman came for the last time and brought two more loaves of bread. The prisoner managed to smuggle the last six watches to another camp where he exchanged them for more bread.

Before we left Mauthausen, we learned from the policeman that of the ten thousand Spanish prisoners brought there in 1940, there were now, in January, 1945, only five hundred remaining. They had been sent, group by group, to the stone quarries. It was impossible to survive the work in the quarries for long because the work was extremely hard and starvation was high.

Chapter 21

MELK

After a few days, our group was sent from Mauthausen to a branch located in a small town near Vienna, Melk. In this large group were seventy-five from the Ukrainian group, including me.

We come down the mountain to the railroad station we had left just a few days before and were loaded into freight cars. Now we went in the opposite direction, eastward, to Melk. Normally it takes only a few hours to go by train from Linz to Vienna, but then it took two days because the railroad had been destroyed in many places by bombing and we had to wait until it was fixed so our freight cars could pass.

Finally we came to Melk. Here the train stopped, all prisoners were ordered off the train, a march column was formed, and, surrounded by SS guards, we walked to the new concentration camp located on a hill not far from the Danube River. We were walking through a beautiful part of the Austrian countryside. I recalled that it was at Melk where the first residence of the Austrian kings was located. Here also was a very old and beautiful monastery. Many other buildings of this now small town looked romantic. On the other hand, the location of the concentration camp looked miserable. Many years before it had been a prison built by Freiherr von Birabo. I don't know how it looked in the Middle Ages, but now it looked more like remains from ancient times.

There was a large rectangle surrounded by a wall and a

double row of electrified fence, in the middle of which was one three-story brick building, the only brick building in the camp. Around it were many very old wooden barracks. I was sent to the first floor of the brick building which housed about seven hundred prisoners. In all, there were about ten thousand prisoners here.

The barracks here, as well as in Auschwitz and Mauthausen, were called blocks. One building was a block, but since here the buildings were of different sizes, the number of prisoners housed in each block varied. The inside of all the buildings, including the brick one, looked worse than the outside; they were never cleaned and never fixed. In every room there were three-story bunks like in the other concentration camps, but even the sleeping arrangements were different from Auschwitz and Mauthausen. Since the prisoners worked in three shifts and at least one-third of the prisoners were always outside the camp, there was no need for everyone to have his own place on the bed. When there was time to sleep, everyone looked for a free bed. Since the time for sleeping was also divided into three shifts according to work, only one-third of the prisoners were sleeping at a time. Therefore, there was, at least theoretically, plenty of room in the beds. The problem was that the worn pallets and broken boards in the beds were never replaced or fixed. When there were broken boards in a bed, the one using the bed simply took the boards from another unused bed for his own. The same thing was done with the pallets. As a result, many beds had only side boards and nothing else. In addition, each bed was supposed to have one blanket for the four prisoners occupying it, but the situation was the same as with the pallets and boards. It was very cold because it was winter and there was no heating in the barracks, so the prisoners took blankets from other beds. It was extremely important to have friends, because if one needed to go to the toilet during the night and had no one to take care of his bed, when he came back, there would be not only no blanket, but also no pallet or boards. Because of that, many of the *musulmen* preferred not to risk leaving their beds during the night. When they had to go to the toilet, they used their own pallets for urinating. The air in the rooms was overpowering.

There was a laundry, but it was extremely small and took

care of only the linen of the SS guards, so the underwear of the prisoners was never cleaned and never changed. Everyone had to wear what he came in wearing for the remainder of the time at Melk.

A bathroom with hot water was located in the brick house, but it was small and often out of order. Once a month the prisoners were taken there to shower naked in their wooden shoes, then they ran naked back to their blocks.

The prisoners at Melk worked basically at building underground roads and tunnels for industry. Because of the continual bombing, German industry had been greatly damaged. The administration had decided to build tunnels in the mountains and transfer the remaining industry to those tunnels for protection.

One of the big places for an industry was built southwest of Vienna. We had to work there for eight hours in three shifts, but the place was quite a distance from the camp, so we had to walk about three miles to the railroad station and then travel about an hour on the train before we arrived at the tunnel. So, in addition to the regular eight hours working in the tunnel, we had two hours spent getting there, two hours going back to the camp, and one hour of waiting after we had returned for checking and so on. Actually, our shift took thirteen hours. There was also a roll call which lasted from one to three hours. Between fourteen and sixteen hours each day a prisoner had to be either working, walking, or standing. Even the travel in the train was exhausting because the freight cars were always overcrowded so that the prisoners had to stand for the whole journey. *Blockältesters, kapos*, and *forarbeiters* were recruited basically as in other camps from the Germans and *Volksdeutsch*. Now, however, no one really cared any more, so that in my *kommando* when a German *kapo* died from old age, a strong Russian prisoner was made *kapo*. There were in other cases *kapos* and *forarbeiters* who were Russian, Polish, or French.

Food was similar to that in Auschwitz and Mauthausen but there was very little possibility for "organizing" additional food because even the *blockältesters* and *kapos* looked like the *musulmen* of Auschwitz in 1944.

The regime here was generally like that in Auschwitz before 1944. Kicking, beating, and killing of prisoners was commonplace and no one cared. Only self-protection gave one a chance to survive.

In our block the *blockältester* was a German criminal from Silesia who spoke a Silesian dialect of Polish. He boasted, being, tall and strong, that he was a boxing champion. No one knew what kind of champion he was—perhaps he was champion in his village or maybe only in his family. Nonetheless he liked to talk about it and every day he selected a prisoner to demonstrate his skills on. He had boxing gloves and selected a prisoner for the "game." With great ceremony he put his gloves on as if he were on a stage, then began to hit the victim. He didn't like the *musulmen* prisoners who fell after the first hit, so he usually selected stronger prisoners who were better able to take the beating. Most fell after three or four hits, and he kicked them as he counted them out.

The most often-used form of punishment here was five to twenty-five lashes. Another kind often used was called *abhangen*. The prisoner was brought under the gallows and told to raise his hands over his head. His hands were bound to the gallows so that he had to stand on his toes. The position was quite uncomfortable, and if a prisoner had to remain that way long, he usually fainted after the first thirty minutes or so. Hanging by his hands, he had to remain until the time was up. Still another kind of punishment was to place the victim in front of the SS office between two rows of electrified barbed wire. There he had to remain at attention under the watch of the SS. It was very cold at this time of year and the prison dress was very light, so the punishment was cruel. It looked at first like the prisoners being punished this way were merely waiting to be called into the office, since one had to wait between the two rows of barbed wire before he was admitted to the office.

The next morning we were taken to the work in the tunnels. It seemed that the work had already been in progress many months because some tunnels had been completed and in two or three places large rooms had been built, and civilian workers were busy there. The prisoners continued building more rooms. With an electric tool some of the prisoners made openings for dynamite, the dynamite was placed and detonated, then the broken stone was loaded on railroad cars and pushed outside and unloaded. The work was very hard and the *kapos* and *forarbeiters* were cruel. There was another administrative post here, that of the *meisters*. These were not prisoners, but civilian specialists who theoretically were only to direct the work professionally and not to interfere with the discipline, but who invariably took advantage of their position of authority and competed with the *kapos* and *forarbeiters* in brutality. Looking on this hard work and beating through the administration in the tunnels I had a clear idea of what the slave work was like in ancient time under the cruel pharaohs.

The work was hard and the march was troublesome to and from the train. The prisoners had to walk by fives, holding each other by their arms very close together. This was to prevent any escape attempt by binding the prisoners to each other. We heard *"Auf gehen"* ("Closer together"), which was abbreviated to *"Auf,"* all the time. It was usually followed by beating when one was not performing to the satisfaction of the *kapo*. This abbreviation, *"Auf,"* the prisoners heard from the time they awakened until the time they fell asleep. On awakening, they heard *"Auf,"* for *"Aufstehen"* ("Stand up"). During the march it was *"Auf gehen,"* and at the train it was *"Auf steigen"* ("Up into the cars"). During the work it was also *"Auf gehen,"* so that all the time there was only *"Auf, auf, auf."* Sarcastically one of the prisoners remarked, "We have heard all the *'aufs'* except *'auf atmen'*('Relax')." It was inconceivable that we would ever hear it with that meaning.

For the first few days I was very uncomfortable because of the biting cold. At Auschwitz I had managed to smuggle some sausage out of the butchery, which I exchanged for a pullover, so this change back to regulation camp dress was very uncomfortable and unaccustomed.

During the work we had to bring sacks of cement and after emptying them I used the paper bags under my clothing to help keep out the cold. This was a definite risk because it was forbidden. When a prisoner was caught doing this, he was given at least five lashes. Fortunately, I was not caught, and tried to stay far away from anyone who might have reason to check. At times when there was a special check, I managed to dispose of the bags. From that experience I found out that paper can be an excellent protection against the cold.

Prisoners were paid here for their work, receiving one mark per week. Pay was made by coupon, and could be exchanged for one pack of cigarettes. For one week of hard work a prisoner could get one pack of cigarettes. This was good, however, for the non-smokers, for we could exchange the cigarettes for additional soup and bread.

One night while going through the camp looking for additional bread or soup to buy, I saw many young boys from ten to sixteen. I was shocked—especially so because since the camp did not have such small clothing, they were given the regular sizes which they somehow managed to keep on their emaciated bodies.

They talked among themselves in Polish, so I asked one of them why there were so many of them and who they were. They told me that they were from Warsaw. At the end of 1944, when the Russian army came to the outskirts of Warsaw, the Polish underground in Warsaw started an uprising. They expected that the Russian army would help from the other side of the Visla River and thus the Germans would be attacked from both sides. However, the Russians didn't want to have to give any of the glory for the liberation of Poland to the Polish people, so they remained on the other side of the river until the uprising had been crushed. While the uprising was going on, there was an offer from the Germans that they would permit, under the oversight of the International Red Cross, the civilians, especially children, to leave the area of the fighting. Their offer was accepted and some thousand children were allowed to go to the Germans. Instead of permitting the children to go to their relatives under the protection of the Red Cross, they were put into German concentration camps. Many, of course, soon died and the rest merely waited to follow them. It was obvious that the German nation had begun to compete with the Russian Communists in treachery and brutality.

Our Ukrainian group had been dispersed to many blocks, but soon we managed to get together again in one block. As I have mentioned, this solidarity was very important to us. We had organized ourselves so that the stronger helped the weaker during the work, and this made a good impression on the guards. They left us much to ourselves as long as we did our work, and usually didn't kick or beat us. Because of this impression, we were all put in a transportation *kommando*, charged with unloading building materials and reloading broken, unused materials back on the cars. It was heavy work, maybe much heavier than that in the tunnels, but it was much healthier because we worked in the fresh air. Even though the ones working inside had occasional opportunities to hide and relax from the continuous work once in a while, the heavy air and lack of sunlight yellowed the skin of these prisoners.

Occasionally there was too much material for our group to handle. Then other prisoners were added. One day there was such a group organized of about twenty prisoners. I was put with them. We were to push a freight car loaded with building material and, in one place, the rail was on a downward grade so that the car would coast down without being pushed. It was necessary, on the contrary, to slow the car down. These new prisoners did not know about slowing the car down, and my shouted warning to them was in vain. The prisoners who had been pushing the car simply let it go. The prisoners who had been pulling the car from in front were too weak to jump aside and were badly hurt when the oncoming car hit them.

Another time we had to unload a long beam from the car. When we twenty prisoners took the beam on our arms, it was so heavy that it was imperative that we push it as hard as we could away from us and jump back. This time, though, some of the prisoners dropped their end too soon and the beam swung around right at me. The beam hit another prisoner first, though, and instead of killing me with the impact, it only struck me lightly in the back. Nevertheless, I felt the effects of the blow for several weeks.

Working in the transport *kommando* with other prisoners randomly selected for it, I saw how cruel some of the *kapos, forarbeiters,* and SS continued to be regardless of the fact that they knew Germany was in its death throes. In my *kommando* was a Russian prisoner who looked rather strong, but probably wasn't. The *forarbeiter* was a Polish *Volksdeutsch* who was very cruel. When he kicked the Russian, the Russian became very angry and said, "Don't hit, you dirty Polish dog, for you

soon will be held responsible for what you are doing here!"
The *forarbeiter* was not brave enough to attack the prisoner
since he was so big and strong-looking, so he called an SS
and told him that this prisoner had insulted the Germans. He
said that the Russian prisoner had told him that in a few more
days the German dogs would be hanged by the victorious
Russian Army. The guard was so enraged that he gave the
Russian an immediate twenty-five lashes. When, at noon, we
had a break for our dinner, the SS came back and gave the
Russian another twenty-five lashes. Fifteen minutes before
our return to camp, the Russian was given the third twenty-
five lashes. He was told that he was to report the next morning to the *forarbeiter* and SS, but he was no longer able to
walk and had to be taken to the hospital. Fortunately, he
found a German male nurse there who was a Communist
political prisoner and took care of him. He reported to the block
administration that the prisoner had died, but actually let him
remain in the *krankenhaus*.

The *kapo* in our *kommando* was a former commissioned officer in the Russian army, a Siberian Mongol, who turned out
to be very friendly, so we had no extra trouble from him. As a
prisoner of war, he had volunteered for the Russian division
in the German army and later, for reasons he didn't reveal to
us, he was arrested and sent here. Although he was a Mongolian Russian citizen, as a former member of the German army,
he was made a *kapo*. He liked the organized discipline of our
group and when, one day, the guards had to move a tower
from a place about one hundred feet from its intended location, he suggested that the Ukrainian group could do it. The
SS guards were eager to find out if we could, and told us that
if we were successful, we would be given a twenty-five-gallon
barrel of soup. It seems unbelievable now that seventy intelligent prisoners would risk their lives in order to get soup, but
our reasons were simple enough. Had we refused the offer,
we could have been ordered to do the work without the reward. In the concentration camps, the prisoners never refused
an opportunity, since refusal was invariably followed by some
kind of punishment. It was, therefore, much more advantageous to accept the proposition while there was promise of a
reward.

As a matter of fact, the other prisoners were not sentimental, either. For instance, one day when we were returning to camp, a stone falling in the tunnel hit and injured a prisoner. Other prisoners had to carry him back to the camp on a stretcher, and I was ordered to help. We put him on the stretcher and walked slowly behind the column. Next to me a Russian prisoner saw that the seemingly dead prisoner, also Russian, had leather shoes, so he slowly unbound them and took them for himself. The wounded prisoner was not yet dead, and when his shoes were taken off, the biting cold awakened him. He looked at us and said, "Don't take my shoes. It is very cold." The one who had taken the shoes answered, "Look at the dirty bum. Already dead and still worrying about shoes. In another hour he will be really warm in the crematorium. After that, in heaven, he will not need any shoes. He should just lie there quietly and not complain." He had no pity for his dying comrade and was afraid that had he not taken the shoes first, someone else would have gotten them.

In the transport *kommando* we had much work to do under the direction of a civilian *meister*, Herr Pajonc. Officially, he should have had no direct contact with the prisoners since his duty was to advise the *kapo* what needed to be done. Actually, though, he behaved as if he were a *kapo* himself. He ordered the prisoners to bring heavy materials from one end of the yard to another and the next day take them back to the former location. All the time he kicked and beat us and forced us to keep to the running tempo in our work. He was an example of the German civilians who, working in the same place as the prisoners, took pleasure in persecuting and torturing the victims of the concentration camps.

One day, when we were returning in the train, a few prisoners opened the door and jumped from the train and escaped. From then on, prisoners were ordered to sit in the cars. Because of the limited space, this was impossible, so only those in front sat down with their hands on their heads. All the rest had to lean over one another. In this position there was no possibility for an escape attempt. It was also a very uncomfortable position to remain in for an hour. The doors were always closed and two SS with machine guns stood in front of the doors.

Very often during the air attacks the railroad was bombed and rails were destroyed. Then a group of prisoners had to repair it. No one cared if the airplanes returned and bombed the prisoners. The survivors simply collected the dead and brought them back to Melk for roll call and counting.

Going to work and back we saw many refugees almost every day. We assumed from this that the end of the war was very near, but our hopes didn't materialize. Two months passed, and once more an evacuation was begun.

At the end of March, we did not go to work. German prisoners were transferred somewhere else or perhaps freed. The *musulmen* were then separated out, put on trucks, given food and told that they would be taken to Mauthausen. They were gassed and brought back to the crematorium. From this we concluded that the stronger prisoners would not be gassed, but would truly be transferred or freed. It seemed that the last days of the Third Reich had finally come.

Chapter 22

EVACUATION ONCE MORE

At the beginning of April the prisoners were ordered to form a march column and received food for a transport. There was a great deal of chaos, so only those in the front of the column received a portion of food. While we were walking toward the Danube River, the symphony of artillery around Vienna was heard. We were brought to the Danube, where we waited for barges used to transport coal. We were loaded on these barges. There was a little room on the top, but it was very cold, so most preferred to go inside although it was very dirty. Soon those who were inside were smeared with coal dust. No one cared and many preferred to go to sleep inside, out of the cold. Both parts of the barges, inside and outside, were overcrowded. There was really no possibility of sleeping. We went westward against the stream, so we progressed very slowly. During the night a few prisoners jumped from the barges into the water. The SS shot at them, but the prisoners were probably successful in their escape because, although there were small boats on both sides of the barges, none of the SS tried to take one and go after the escapees. The SS realized that there was the danger of partisans or advance detachments of the Russian army being on the banks. Of course, only a skilled swimmer could risk such an escape, especially since the water was extremely cold.

After four days we arrived at Linz. We expected to be taken back to Mauthausen, however, the barge did not stop on the right bank of the Danube, but on the left. We were ordered off the barge and onto the bank. Now we continued on foot. We were informed that we would have to walk about ten miles. Because the area around Linz had been devastated by air raids we would then be loaded on trains and taken someplace in the Alps. We were given a portion of food— each prisoner was given about forty decagrams of bread, five decagrams of margarine and five decagrams of horse meat sausage. Some prisoners ate half and left the other half for later, but most ate it all immediately because, as we left the barges, we had seen some military kitchens being loaded on trucks. We expected that they would be taken to the place where the train was waiting for the prisoners, and dinner would be prepared—soup would be waiting for us there. However, when, after about four hours of marching, we stopped at midday there was neither train nor kitchen. We received no soup or anything else to eat. We could relax only for a few minutes. Those who had saved half their food ate it; the others could only watch. After a few minutes, the order "Auf" came and we reformed the column and continued to walk.

We walked until nightfall with no additional food. On this day we saw quite a contrast between the Czech population we met while we were walking from Auschwitz to Mauthausen two or three months before and the Austrian-German population here. We passed the villages, but when the hungry and thirsty prisoners asked for something to eat or drink, they were not heard. The people watched us, but no one was willing to help. Overnight we stopped at a farm. Here there were two or three barns and a big yard. Some prisoners were lucky enough to find a place inside the barns, but most had to sleep outside on the ground. After a few hours of lying on frozen ground, there was a great deal of water beneath us. No one cared—of utmost importance was being able to relax, regardless of the conditions.

In the morning we were awakened and once again received nothing to eat or drink. We continued to walk. After the second day, when we stopped once more, we were given some tea. Our hopes went up, because we took that as a sign that we would soon be getting food. Soon we found out that the tea had not been prepared for the prisoners; it was simply too much for the SS, and since they didn't need any more, they decided to give the remainder to the prisoners. There was no further food.

As a matter of fact, from Linz to Ebensee was not far, and there was a good straight road between the two towns. However, the main road was overcrowded with refugees and military transports, and it was often strafed by American aircraft. Because of this, the prisoners were not taken along the regular road, but mostly traveled small roads and streets, zigzagging from one side to another, occasionally even backtracking. Even on these small roads there was sometimes an air attack. We experienced one on our second day of walking and had to go into a forest about two hundred yards from the road until the attack was over.

Walking on the fourth class, or smaller, road was very difficult because there was not enough room to keep in the lines the guards wanted. From time to time we would meet a farmer's cart loaded with hay and there would be confusion as to how we should pass. The whole transport would be stopped, a single line formed, and the guards surrounded it with their machine guns. This was why it took so unbelievably long to travel this short distance.

I have spoken of our march from Linz to Ebensee, but actually, at this time no one knew where we were going.

The third day after we left the barges seven days since we had left Melk, we continued to walk without any food or drink.

That night we were brought into the big courtyard of a brewery. Here we slept on the ground. The courtyard was surrounded by a low wall. On one side there were the buildings of the brewery and on another side was the monastery. The nuns watched us from the windows of the monastery and we indicated that we were hungry and thirsty, that we would like something to eat or drink. The guards warned the nuns that helping the prisoners was forbidden. Neither then nor during the night did the nuns try to throw bread through the window, although it would not have been difficult. None of the guards cared enough to pay any attention to who had thrown the bread. Even if the German nuns had sympathy for the concentration camp prisoners, they did nothing to show it. They, too, obeyed the orders of the Nazis.

In the early afternoon of the third day of our march, we were passed by two trucks bringing *kapos* and *forarbeiters* from Melk. They didn't take part in our march, but had been left there with the SS guards to complete the evacuation of the camp. After this was finished, they were loaded into trucks and taken to the new camp. Because the road we were walking on was narrow, we had to make a line and the trucks had to pass by very slowly and carefully. Therefore, there was some opportunity to exchange conversation with the *kapos* and *forarbeiters*. One sentence, "Melk is *kaput*," told us that Vienna must be occupied by the Russian army since Melk was located about a dozen miles west of Vienna. If Melk were occupied, then Vienna must have been occupied also. This was good news for us; we hoped that now the war would not last more than one or two weeks.

One of the guards in the trucks with the *kapos* and *forarbeiters* threw packages of crackers to us. I am not sure how many packages he threw, but one fell right in the middle of our group. We divided it among our friends. Each one received only one thin piece of these crackers. which were American crackers. We had never seen any like them before. Each piece was perforated so that it consisted of nine very small pieces. Someone explained that this was a scientifically made piece of bread extract; one 2 by 3-inch piece was equal in quality to one kilogram of bread and ten decagrams of butter. We consumed the cracker very carefully. We broke it onto the small portions, convincing ourselves that each little piece equaled almost ten decagrams of bread. This small cracker lasted us for a whole meal on the third day and another meal on the next day. Psychologically, the story about the quality of the crackers worked.

On the fourth day we continued to walk without even any water. Many prisoners fell from exhaustion but, hard to believe though it may be, there were much fewer falling now—even though we had been walking for four days without food and water—than had fallen when we were evacuated from Auschwitz with food and in much better physical condition. The prisoners who fell now were not killed as they had been during our evacuation from Auschwitz. They were left behind for the trucks following to pick up and take someplace, probably a hospital or concentration camp.

We passed Gmunden, and continued to walk along the road beside Lake Ebensee. The country was beautiful. Along the one side was a long, narrow lake and on the other were high mountains. It looked magnificent, but I don't think any of the prisoners enjoyed the scenery; everyone was involved in thinking how long they could continue to walk.

A prisoner walking beside me complained greatly on the first day. "It is impossible to survive," he said. "No one can survive. If one does survive, it will be impossible to find room for all of us in another camp and we will be immediately put into the gas chambers. We should resign ourselves to the last days of our lives."

At the beginning, I tried to persuade him that it was not so bad and that we had no more than one or two weeks to wait before the war would be over. My arguments were to no effect. I finally became angry and told him, "Look, before you fall down and die or are put in a gas chamber, I will kill you if you don't stop complaining and change your position."

"Why?" he said. "I haven't said anything against you. I am only talking about our situation. Why do you want to kill me?"

"Well," I said, "because I would like to eat a piece of your flesh, so you had better change your place."

He looked at me as if I had lost my mind, and moved to another place.

I was glad to get rid of him because his complaining continued, and it made me more nervous than the hunger and exhaustion. Only by concentrating on what hope we had were we able to continue, and the constant talk of dying or being sent to a gas chamber was unnerving.

We were in the high mountains and although it was April, there was still much snow. Sometimes we got snow and used it for water.

In the early afternoon of the fourth day we got a break. There was a place between the rocks and we were allowed to sit down for about thirty minutes, then we were ordered to get up and continue walking. Only a few were able to stand. The guards' clubbing of the prisoners didn't help. Many who jumped up when they were hit fell down again. Since the majority were unable to walk, the guards changed their minds. We were allowed to continue sitting or lying on the ground. A car was sent from the camp at Ebensee about an hour later with bread. Everyone was given a pound of bread. Unfortunately, the bread was of the worst quality, and the prisoners had been four days without food. It was, therefore, dangerous to eat too much of it at one time. We were told to eat slowly, but in many cases the warning was to no avail. Some ate all the bread immediately. Among these were two of my friends—a young painter, Ciuman, and a theology student, Marchycky. They disregarded the warning and ate the whole loaf of bread; they were struck by stomach convulsions and were soon dead. At least a hundred others died the same way.

Chapter 23

EBENSEE

Late in the afternoon of our fourth day of marching we passed the little town of Ebensee and went to a small concentration camp by the same name located on top of the hill some
miles outside the town.

The small camp consisted of twenty wooden barracks
built in a forest. The only brick building was the crematorium,
and actually only a part of it was brick. The other part, used
for keeping corpses, was wooden. The rectangle, as in all
other cases, was surrounded by double electrified wire and a
high wall with towers for the SS guards and their machine
guns. In front of the gate was a place for the roll call. We
went through the normal procedure, but after we had showered and had had come into the barracks there was not
enough clothing available. Only a part received all items of
prisoners' clothing; the others received some of the items. The
last group received no clothing at all and had to wait a few
days naked. I was in this last group and had only a blanket to
ward off the cold.

The next day the prisoners were ordered to go to work,
but only those who had clothing could do that. The others
had to remain in the blocks. One group of prisoners was sent
to repair the bombed railroad and when the administration
saw that there were not enough fully dressed prisoners, they
began to collect others from among those who had only one

piece of clothing to complete the work group of one hundred.

Prisoners began to hide what they had—shirt or pants—on the beds. This was discovered and about one hundred needed prisoners were sent to the work with full sets of clothing made up from pieces found on the beds. Those who had to remain in the block were brought outside for punishment exercises. We were taken back into the blocks, but the windows were opened and there we had to remain naked for two or three hours as punishment for trying to hide our pieces of clothing.

On the third day I received a shirt and on the fifth day I was given pants and a coat and was sent to the work. The basic work here was the same as it was in Melk—to build tunnels and rooms for underground industry.

In the bed I was assigned I found a hidden pullover, but since it was too dangerous to wear it in the normal way, I decided to use it to replace the underwear I did not have and wore it under my pants.

After I received my pants and coat I was added to a *kommando* working in the construction of tunnels. The *kommando* was called Holzmann-Polensky.

KZ Ebensee was one of the branches of concentration camp Mauthausen, but we met something new here—a real famine. In all concentration camps the prisoners received a starvation portion of food, but always there was the chance to organize something additional, and prisoners were given at least one-third of what a regular worker would need to survive. Here the situation was totally different. We received virtually no food. In the morning when we had to go to work, we were given only tea or coffee. It wasn't real tea or coffee, just a drink made from tree leaves or something else. It was at least hot. There was nothing more than that in the morning.

At noon we were given a portion of "soup." However, in other camps what we were given was really soup, but here it was only the hot water in which the potatoes for the SS guards had been boiled. After the potatoes were ready, they were taken out for the SS and the prisoners received only this hot water with sometimes a piece of potato in it. That was our entire lunch.

Between 6:00 and 7:00 P.M. there was again one portion

of coffee or tea and a portion of bread. A one-kilogram loaf was divided among twelve prisoners. It was made from extremely bad ingredients. It was impossible to cut it into twelve pieces, so they cut it into four. The prisoners were divided into groups of three. One got the one-quarter loaf and had to divide it for himself and the other two prisoners in his group. The prisoners had no knife, but even if they had had a very good knife, the bread still would have been impossible to cut. However, as we had done in the prison at Montelupich, we of the Ukrainian group tried to divide it evenly. In the other groups, though, usually the strongest prisoner would take the whole portion and run away with it to eat it all himself. The two others would not receive even this small portion of bread. As a result, an average of five hundred prisoners died each day from starvation.

There was a *schonungsblock*, a recuperation section of the hospital, meant for prisoners too ill or exhausted to work. There they were to stay until they had recuperated enough to return to the work, but actually it was the place where the prisoners finished their lives. It was one of the wooden barracks where there were no beds. The prisoners brought by others were placed on the floor. Here they remained until they died. They lay on the floor unable to stand and received the same portion of food as all the others—almost nothing, so there was no chance for recovery. When one died, the portion of bread that was to have been his was given to the *stubendienst* and *blockältester*, so that often they did not take the dead out for three or four days and continued to report them as alive during that time.

This was the last concentration camp in the territory still in operation at that time—the others had already been liberated by the American or English armies in the west and north or by the Russian army in the east. From all camps the prisoners who had been evacuated before the camps were liberated were brought here. As a result, at least five hundred new prisoners were brought in to replace the five hundred who had died from starvation and perhaps two hundred more who had died during the work.

In Mauthausen, after evacuation from Auschwitz, our Ukrainian group was separated. Only a part was sent to Melk.

The others were sent to other branches of Mauthausen. One group had been sent immediately to Ebensee. Now we found them mostly in the *schonungsblock*; only a few were still able to work and many had already died.

A good friend of mine was in the *schonungsblock*, so I visited him after work. He was lying on the floor, unable to even lift his head to greet me. He only glanced at me and told me that he would not ever leave, that he would die in the next hour. He begged me to ask the administration to remove the prisoners on either side of him who had been dead for three and four days. I asked the *stubendienst*, but he told my friend to be patient for a few more hours; he would soon join them so it shouldn't make any difference to him that there were dead men beside him.

The conditions during the work were about the same as they were in Melk. *Kapos* and *forarbeiters* continued to find pleasure in kicking and beating the prisoners. The only difference was that in Auschwitz, and to some degree in Melk, when a prisoner fell down and was unable to get up, the *kapo* or *forarbeiter* put his knees against the prisoner's throat to finish him. Here in Ebensee this was not done. Instead, when a prisoner was unable to stand up, two other prisoners were ordered to take him to the *schonungsblock*.

Here also, as in Melk, were the civilian *meisters*. They interfered here, also, in the work of the prisoners, kicking and beating them with obvious pleasure.

In the *kommando* where I worked there was a man called *Meister* Barany. I heard his name when another *meister* called him Herr Barany. Very often during the work we experienced a blackout because the lighting was only temporary and when someone touched the wires it caused a blackout. So once when we had a long blackout, Herr Barany was near me in the darkness. I took advantage of the fact that he could not see us and said, "We are just as human as you and the others. Here is a former French general, here is a priest, here is a former Polish professor, I have a higher education, too, and there are intelligent people from all over Europe in this group. Why do you keep on torturing, persecuting, and beating us? The war is almost over. Can you not be humane even for this short time?"

He answered, "Well, you are right, but I am not responsible for all that is going on. You must realize that I am an Austrian and Austria is occupied by Germany as are your countries. I am not responsible for National Socialistic Germany and I will be glad, too, when Austria is liberated. I never had anything against non-German people."

Then the lights came on, and as soon as there was light in our section he shouted to us, "*An die arbeit!*" This means "To the work." He began hitting the prisoners with his stick once more. What he had said in the darkness was only a trick because he was afraid that one of the prisoners might take advantage of the darkness to kill him. Actually, even though he was Austrian, he was just as sadistic and brutal to the non-German prisoners as were the Germans themselves.

The terrible hunger forced the prisoners to try to eat grass and charcoal. This had already been done in Auschwitz, but here it took place much more often. It was the general belief that German margarine was extracted from charcoal chemically. This meant that in charcoal there was a percentage of margarine and if one ate some charcoal one might force the stomach to do what the specialists did in making margarine. Almost all the prisoners brought to the *schonungsblock* had black lips from eating charcoal. Of course, this didn't work and only caused additional suffering and stomach pains.

One Russian prisoner working in my *kommando* told me that he and three of the other prisoners, one Polish and two French, decided to eat the flesh of one of the new prisoners. During the night they killed him and ate his flesh. The result was that they had stomach convulsions. He survived, but the other three had died. He said he would never try eating human flesh again.

Two of the prisoners in my *kommando* were Hungarian Jews. One of them told me that they had been students before they were arrested. They both spoke fluent German. Only one now talked; the other didn't react to anything. When the *forarbeiter* and *meister* were in another part of the corridor and couldn't see us, we stopped working to conserve our energy. The other young Jewish prisoner continued to work. I tried to tell him that he should not continue because he would soon fall down from exhaustion. There was absolutely no reaction.

Then I told him that for his work he would get nothing additional to eat. "Eat, eat," he said. "Yes," I said. "The small portion of bread will not get larger." "Bread, bread!" he shouted. I found out that only when he heard the words connected with food did he react. Otherwise, he showed no awareness of what was going on around him.

Every day when we returned from the work, at least one-quarter of the *kommando* were delivered as dead to the crematorium or to the *schonungsblock*, starved and exhausted. They were replaced the next morning by others, since bringing of prisoners from the other camps continued.

One day I helped deliver my friend Lux, the one who had stood on his head in the prison in Krakau, and the brothers Rowanchuk. Once they had been tall, strong, young boys from the Carpathian Mountains. The older one was especially strong, and when he worked in the butchery in Auschwitz the SS liked for him to demonstrate his strength. He would take one hundred kilograms of meat from the floor and put it on a table. Now he was only skin and bones, weighing no more than seventy pounds and no longer able to stand on his feet. In order that these friends would not be subjected to the kicking, I helped them go to the *schonungsblock*. Two days later when I went to visit them, I found that they were already dead.

One of the new prisoners, a young Polish political prisoner, told me an interesting story about his experiences in Gardelegen. During the evacuation of the concentration camp where he was a prisoner they were walking in different directions because of the confusion caused by the military operations. In the second week of April, 1945 they came to a village, Gardelegen, near Magdeburg. The *kommandant* of the transport, along with the mayor of the town, ordered all prisoners to go into a big wooden barn. About one thousand prisoners were crowded into the barn, then the doors were locked and the wooden building set on fire. The prisoners tried to break down the door, but most of them were soon suffocated by the smoke. Only a few were able to break through the doors or wooden walls, but when they tried to run out they were met with machine guns. Not more than ten from a group of more than one thousand escaped. After one day, since they were in prison dress, they were caught by villagers and reported to German authorities. Since another transport was then passing the place, they were added to the new transport and taken to Ebensee. He also told us about the conditions in the camp where he had been before, and especially about the SS guard Ziereis. He was the moral double of Palitsch in Auschwitz. He liked to torture the prisoners, and so, when his fourteen-year-old son had a birthday, he gave him a special birthday gift. He gave him a gun and forty prisoners. The forty victims were taken to an orchard and bound to the trees for the fourteen-year-old boy to use for target practice. After the war, during the trial of this beast, his son was a witness and admitted that this had actually happened.

One day during the roll call I noticed a small group of about ten prisoners brought separately to the roll call by two SS guards and then taken away separately again. They were unbelievably healthy and well-dressed. They wore the usual prisoners' dress, but it was clean and they had pullovers and shirts under their coats. From a distance I saw on one of them the triangle with an "F" on it. I was uncertain what to think because I had thought that they must have been German prisoners working in a special part of the administration, but the "F" indicated that this was not the case. I asked the other prisoners who these were, and found out that the "F" designated a special *kommando*. One who knew about it told me that they belonged to a *kommando* where it was easier for them to make money than to let them go. I thought a minute and asked him if that meant they were counterfeiters and he told me that was right. They forged not only money but also documents. These were the best forgers selected from criminals all over Europe. They had worked for a long time forging pounds, dollars, and other currencies and all kinds of documents needed for the Gestapo or military intelligence or counter-intelligence. They had been brought here because there was now no other place safe enough for them to continue their work.

A prisoner who had been transferred from Buchenwald told us about a German female beast, Ilse Koch. She was the wife of the *kommandant* of Buchenwald. Taking advantage of the position of her husband, she often visited the concentration camp and selected prisoners for her own purposes—material for bookbinding and sexual entertainment. When she found a prisoner with good skin, she had a certain type of tattoo made on his body. When the tattoo was ready, the prisoner was killed, his skin was removed, prepared, and used for binding the books in her private collection. Her whole collection of books was bound in human skin. Also, it seems that she was abnormal both sexually and psychologically. When she saw a new prisoner, well built and handsome, she told her husband that the prisoner had insulted her by looking at her lustfully. Her husband allowed her to choose the punishment for such a prisoner, so she had the unfortunate prisoner taken by a guard to her room. There he was undressed and forced to have sexual relations with her. Then she had the guard bind him to the wall and she beat him with a club on his genitals until he was dead. His body was taken to the crematorium.

All information we received from the new prisoners arriving each day indicated that we were in the last stage of the war, the last weeks, or maybe even the last days. Nevertheless, in these last days, the question of whether "to be or not to be" was extremely acute for all of us. We were exhausted and each day more and more prisoners died.

Also, as we had passed the town Ebensee, we saw on the wall in big letters, *"Der Teufel hat ihn geholt"* ("The devil caught him"). At first, because it was in such large letters, I and the others thought that it had been written about Hitler. When we got closer, we saw additional wording to the effect that it was about Roosevelt. *"Erst jetzt der krieg beginns"* ("Now we will start a real war"). It was not clear to us what that meant, but some suspected that the Germans had developed an atomic bomb and would destroy England, Russia, and America with it. This would have been a critical turn in the war and could have caused the war to last many more months.

We wondered still what would happen in the last moments to the prisoners. We all knew that the end of the war was near, and wondered what our fate would be. We often heard that the government of Nazi Germany had made the decision that no non-German prisoners should be permitted to survive and report to others after the war what had happened in the concentration camps. To us this was logical. We had been transferred from Auschwitz to Mauthausen, from Mauthausen to Melk, and from Melk here to Ebensee, but we knew we had reached the end of the line. Ebensee was the last camp in the Reich. Here the final decision about non-German prisoners still alive would be made.

We Ukrainian political prisoners had something additional to worry about. If the camp were liberated before the Germans annihilated all prisoners, who would liberate Ebensee? Would it be the Americans or English from the south or the Russians from the east? If the English or Americans came, we would be safe; if the Russians liberated the camp we knew the Ukrainian political prisoners would be sent to Russian concentration camps or executed—we were their political enemies, too. We were political enemies of Communist Russia as well as Nazi Germany.

During the first week of May, 1945 the news spread that Hitler was dead. Someone who had managed to get a German newspaper told us that the Führer had fallen in heavy battle against the Russians in Berlin. True or untrue, the news brought none of the expected changes. Everything continued as it had for the next two or three days.

On the morning of May 4 the roll call was different. The *kommandant* of the camp and the SS guards were absent. In their place was a civilian who introduced himself to us as the mayor of the town Ebensee. He told us that the war was over, we were free, and were under the protection of the International Red Cross. He said that he was responsible for us. He also told us that there was some danger that some diehard Nazis might decide to make a last stand here in the only part of Germany not occupied by the Allies. In that case, he told us, we would be in danger since the camp might be strafed. He suggested that we all take cover in the tunnels we had built for two or three days until an allied army would come to take charge of us.

We all reacted suspiciously and nervously to his suggestion. Only a few days earlier we had been ordered to bring bags of dynamite and put them on both sides of the entrance to the tunnels. Many bags were placed in other places inside the tunnels. Therefore, we feared that what the mayor was suggesting was nothing more than a trick—that when we were all in the tunnels we would be buried there by the explosion of the dynamite. We told him that if we had to die, we would die where we were.

To our surprise, the mayor didn't insist, but told us that it was only his idea for our well-being. If we wanted to stay in camp, he would have food brought to us here.

In addition, he told us that everything would go on as before; there would be guards at the gate and on the walls. The difference would be that these guards would be for the purpose of protecting the prisoners from the last bands of Nazis, SS, who were still operating in the mountains in the area.

After the roll call we were not sent to work, but were allowed to stay in the camp and do whatever we wanted.

We saw that there were no longer any SS guards at the towers. In their places were members of the *Volkssturm*, the militia. The gate was locked. None of the prisoners were permitted to leave the camp. We were informed that these regulations had been imposed by the International Red Cross which had a representative who would come to the camp soon and take it over.

At noon, instead of the usual hot water, we were given real soup, a gruel. This was the first we had had in three weeks. Then we had to wait until night.

For part of the time I walked around, but that was not so easy because I, also, was totally exhausted. However, I wanted to see those from my group who were still alive to find out what we should do. I met some of them and we decided that as soon as the gates were .opened, we would leave and find out what our true situation was. In case it was not possible for us to leave the camp, we would all pretend to be Polish, Czech, or Russian from the first moment until we were sure we were out of reach of the Russian NKVD.

For supper, between 5:00 and 6:00 P.M., we received another bowl of real soup.

There was no other roll call that day or thereafter.

For breakfast the next morning we were given some coffee and some real bread.

At noon and again at supper we were given bowls of real soup.

Spring had come to the mountains and it was warm, pleasant weather. The prisoners who were able walked around, nervously waiting for the final conclusion to our situation. We still feared that we might be annihilated. It was known that some of the *kapos* and *blockältesters* had managed to leave the camp, and this added to our suspicions that something might yet happen to us.

On Sunday, May 6, 1945, about 10:00 A.M., a shouting came from the prisoners who were looking through the gate. They shouted that a tank was coming. Soon a tank appeared on the narrow road, broke down the gate, and came into the camp. On top of the tank were two or three soldiers waving and smiling at the prisoner. From all sides the prisoners jumped on the tank, shouting happily, thanking them for our liberation, kissing the soldier and the tank. From where I stood I saw that there was a star on the side of the tank. I did not know then that the Americans, too, used a five-pointed star, and so I thought that that it was a Russian tank. So I decided to take advantage of the open gate and I left the camp quickly.

Other prisoners were streaming through the gate toward the barracks where the kitchen for the SS had been located. The prisoners broke into the building and went looking for food. In chaos everyone tried to get whatever he could find. I got an onion which I ate whole, then found a piece of bread and ate that, too. A barrel of butter was opened, and I, along with many others, tried to put my hand in the barrel. One tried to cut out some butter with a knife he had found and wounded many prisoners in the process. In only a few moments the barrel was empty. When everything had been eaten, the prisoners went back to the camp, counting on the help of the liberators.

I met another Ukrainian prisoner and we decided to try to get to the next town. When we came out on the road which led to the town of Ebensee, we were passed by a girl on a bicycle. We stopped her, asking for something to eat. She was frightened and told us that she had only a piece of bread, opened her bag, and gave it to us. She left quickly, happy that we had let her go. When we examined the bread, we were surprised to find that it looked exactly like *Paska*, a kind of bread prepared by Ukrainians for Easter. My friend said that the day was Sunday, Easter according to the Ukrainian calendar. We thought perhaps that the girl was a Ukrainian working as a slave somewhere in the neighborhood in German industry. At any rate we happily consumed the *Paska*, looked at the concentration camp behind us, and recalled the words of the Ukrainian poet, Iwan Franko. In his poem about the abolition of serfdom he wrote, "Oh, Lord, since the world existed, there never was such a happy Easter."

We were quite overcome with happiness, realizing that we had survived four years in a Nazi concentration camp and all this inferno was now behind us. The Nazi German Empire which, according to Goebbels, was to have lasted one thousand years, had ceased to exist and we who were to have been annihilated had outlived the "thousand-year Nazi empire."

During the time we were looking for food in the SS kitchen, I had found some big scales. I had checked my weight and found that I weighed 70 pounds, a little less than half my regular weight of 155 to 160 pounds. It didn't matter now, however, for the important thing was that I was alive, the war was over and the concentration camp was behind.

After walking for about an hour, we decided to rest, and sat down on some rocks. About an hour later we were joined by a third Ukrainian prisoner who had left the camp alone. We three continued to walk to Gmunden, the next large town.

Chapter 24

LIBERATION AND ITS AFTERMATH

The German Third Reich had ceased to exist, but what would it be replaced by? What would happen politically in the countries formerly under German occupation? And what would all this mean to us personally? The answer to all these questions could be found only with the well-informed Ukrainians, so we traveled to Gmunden, where we expected to find some other Ukrainian refugees.

On the way to Gmunden we had to pass the town of Ebensee. We left the concentration camp with the impression that the tank which had entered the camp was Russian. Therefore, we were afraid to use the main road through Ebensee in case we should meet a detachment of the Russian army. We decided to pass on the outskirts along a small road.

We were hungry and wanted to find something to eat, so we went to the first farmer's house we saw. We found that there was no farmer there, only his wife and children. We asked her to give us something to eat, explaining that we had just left the concentration camp. From her first look at us, she must have known that we were on the brink of starvation. However, she gave us nothing, explaining that she was very short of food and had to think first of getting something for her small children. She told us that even though she sympathized with us, she was unable to help. She said that this was the first time she had heard of a concentration camp and that she hadn't realized there were any concentration camps anywhere in Germany, much less here at Ebensee.

I was prepared to accept her explanation and leave, but one of my friends got angry and said that he wanted to talk to her in a different language. He went into the kitchen and, taking a butcher knife in his hand, said in broken, rough German, "Me in concentration camp. Me hungry. Me not die. You die. Your children die. I need eat food. Food." The woman was terrified and although she was much stronger than all of us together, she was afraid of the knife. She fell to her knees and pleaded with him not to kill her or the children and said that she would give us what we wanted. She took us to the basement where there was plenty of food. To us it was like looking in a grocery. We took some food, made some coffee, and continued on our journey.

Thus our first contact with the civilian German population here in Austria did nothing to raise our estimate of Germans. These first people we met pretended not to know of the existence of the concentration camps and the atrocities committed by the Nazis, even though they must have seen the camps every day. Even after the liberation, they didn't want to help the victims of the Nazis by giving them food.

Soon we met another prisoner sitting beside the road just outside the village, he, too was Ukrainian, so our group grew to four.

After about an hour of walking, we passed a farmhouse with a big courtyard surrounded by a high fence. We rang the bell on the gate and a woman appeared and asked what we wanted. We told her that we would like something to eat and some clothes—especially shirts—since what we had had not been changed for a month. She told us, angrily, that she could not help us, that she was in no way responsible for what had happened to us, and that we could not come into her house because we had lice and she didn't want us bringing an epidemic to her family. She told us to move on and get someone else to help us. She brought a big dog from the house and let it run loose in the courtyard. The dog jumped at the gate and barked, so we decided to continue our walk.

After another hour we came to a railroad station. The railroad was not operable because American bombs in the last days had cut the tracks in many places. There were many freight cars in the station, and we decided to check them for anything that might be of use to us. One car was closed, and when we opened the door we were surprised to find it full of cans of lard. There was so much lard there that it would have been enough to supply a concentration camp for a week. As we opened the boxes, two civilian guards, militiamen, came and told us to leave immediately. They took the cans we had and told us that this was military food and had been taken over by the American army. No one was allowed to bother it, they insisted.

We asked them to help us by giving us clothes and food, but they told us that all prisoners should remain in the concentration camps and be taken care of by the International Red Cross. They could not help us, they told us, because they had to stay near the cars and could not leave to get us anything.

We left the station and continued on our journey to Gmunden. We realized that had our friend not intimidated the German housewife outside Ebensee, we would have walked from Ebensee to Gmunden without anything to eat. We got no help from people living close to the road between the two towns.

Soon we were passed by a military jeep. The driver wanted to pick us up. He asked us to get into the car. We were confused because, although he spoke in English, we saw the five-pointed star on the jeep. We were unsure whether he were Russian or American, and decided not to take the chance. "Come on French, Belgian," he invited once more.

"No, not French. Not Belgian. We are Polish," said one who knew a little English.

"All right, come on Polish," he said.

The friend replied, "Not just Polish, but Ukrainian-Polish."

"OK, OK," insisted the American.

Finally we found a way to refuse the invitation. The boy pointed to his stomach and said, "We no good, no good." He started to take off his belt.

"Oh, I see," the American said and drove off.

Soon we arrived at Gmunden and went to the police station immediately. We found that instead of the Nazi police there was now an Austrian militia. It was the same men, but in different uniform and under a different name—"Militia of Liberated Austria." When they saw us, they told us that we, as well as all other surviving prisoners of the German concentration camps, were under the protection of the International Red Cross and should remain in the camp. There, they told us, we would receive everything we needed until our representatives came and took us back to our countries.

We refused to go back and told them that we were looking for a Ukrainian refugee to provide us with some information. One of the men said that he knew a Ukrainian doctor in the hospital there by the name of Pasichnak. He told us that they would take us there. The commander of the militia liked that idea and told his secretary to make a note that four former prisoners from the concentration camp Ebensee were delivered to the hospital for checkups and treatment.

We were taken to the hospital. The doctor was glad to see us and was very friendly. He went to his room and brought some of his clothing for us to wear. He had a room prepared for us and sent us to the washroom with chemicals for our disinfection. Then we were told to remain in the room so that we might be given careful checkups. He said that we must be very careful not to eat too much because our stomachs would rebel after all we had been through. He also gave us some information about the general political situation.

We found that the war was really over and that Germany was occupied by Americans, French, and English in the west and south and by the Russians in the east. Here where we were was under the American occupation. The beginning of the Russian occupation was about twenty miles north. He explained to us that we had no need to fear the five-pointed star on trucks and cars because it was the symbol of the American military and had nothing to do with the Russian government. Russian vehicles carried a red star. He told us, laughingly, that we should especially like the American military police because their cars carried two lines—blue and yellow—just like the Ukrainian national flag. According to his understanding, the national center for Ukrainian political prisoners was Munich in Bavaria. There, he heard, a Ukrainian committee had been organized. He told us that we should go there to get all the information we needed from members of the committee.

We remained in the hospital about a week. The doctor reported us to the International Red Cross and a new international organization, the UNRRA, which took care of political refugees. We soon received packages and had plenty of food. On the advice of the physician, we began to eat very carefully and slowly. He told us how much we should eat each time and we ate eight times daily in the controlled amounts. The doctor took the rest of the food away. The first day this was a real problem because it was hard to control our appetites, and none of us wanted to stop eating. We found, though, that it was extremely important to our health that we do this, and we gained strength each day. After the week in the hospital, we felt strong enough to continue our journey. It would have been better for us had we remained another month, but we were anxious for political information. We wanted to know what was going on in Ukraine, in the world, and in Germany. We could find out nothing in Gmunden, so we decided to go on to Munich. Transportation was not yet in service, so it was necessary to walk a few more days to reach a main railroad connection between Linz, Salzburg, and Munich.

Leaving Gmunden, we came to a camp for forced laborers from Ukraine. We had received the information that such a camp existed from Dr. Pasichnak. We were eager to meet the Ukrainians there. We found that this camp was for girls, about three hundred from eastern Ukraine. Their leader had been a high school teacher. She told us that they were preparing to go back. They had already been visited by a representative of the Russian government and had been told that transportation would be available for them. We couldn't understand why they were all prepared to go back and surrender to the Russian government, but the teacher explained their problem to us. She told us that they all hated the Russian government and wanted to stay, but they knew there was no guarantee that they could remain. They all feared that had they chosen to remain here, that they would have been deported anyway and dealt with even more harshly for trying to stay away from Russia.

She told us that she had been born under the Communist regime of proletarian parents. She had been a small child in 1932-33, but old enough to understand what was going on. She remembered the horrible smell of the people of her village dying of starvation. Among those who had died were her mother and father. She had been taken from the village and given to a government orphanage, and educated in the Communist ideology, but she could never forget the horrible "famine" organized by the Communists in 1932-33.

All the girls in the group were from Vinnytsa and the villages surrounding it. Because we had been in the concentration camps since 1941, we had not heard the story of Vinnytsa. She told us about it.

Behind the building used by the KNVD, the Russian police, in Vinnytsa, there was a big courtyard cut off from the streets by a high wooden fence. Shortly before the war, the fence was torn down and a park was established. When Vinnytsa was occupied by the German Army, they decided to remove the statue of Stalin in the middle of the park and build something for military use. When the Ukrainian workers began to dig around the statue to remove it, they found, to their horror, skeletons of people who had been murdered in the previous courtyard. Under the supervision of the German authorities, the ground was searched and about ten thousand skeletons of victims of the NKVD were discovered. Their bloody shirts told the story of the horrible torture they had undergone before they had died. The whole courtyard was nothing more than a hidden cemetery. Over the bodies, the Soviets had built a park. Many of the victims were still recognizable to their relatives from their clothing. It was discovered, therefore, that the prisoners arrested by the Soviet Russian authorities at the end of the 1930s and early 1940s were not sent to Siberia as their families had been told, but had been tortured to death and buried here. Thus in one small city, Vinnytsa, there were about ten thousand victims of the Soviet Russian brand of terror. Similar things had happened in each city of Ukraine.

She said had they known they would have protection from the Americans, they would have remained as would have the millions of others brought to Germany as slave labor. However, they felt that if they voluntarily returned to the Soviets, they might be allowed to return to their villages. On the other hand, they were afraid that had they chosen to remain and then were forced to return by the Americans or Germans, they would be immediately sent to the concentration camps in Siberia. It was for this cause, according to the teacher, that they preferred to return voluntarily. Later I asked a German official if it were possible to remain if one refused to return to Russia. He told me that according to an agreement between the United States and Russia, all the citizens of the USSR were obliged to return. Those who refused to return voluntarily would be forced to go back.

We ourselves had no idea of what our situation was now after the capitulation of the Nazis, so we could not make any suggestions to these girls about their actions. We promised, nevertheless, to find out when we came into contact with the Ukrainian committee if there were any way to help them. With broken hearts, we continued our journey.

Before sunset we came to a German farm. The farmer allowed us to sleep on the hay in his barn, but said that if we wanted to get some milk and butter for supper and breakfast we must give him coupons, because he had to deliver them according to government regulation. He had to show that he had given some of his milk and butter to former political prisoners. Before we had left Gmunden, we had been given coupons by the German police. Because we had been given some food by the American Red Cross, we still had some of our coupons. We gave the proper number to the farmer. Since we had no money, we offered to pay him for the food with a double portion of the coupons. He was glad to accept our offer because, as we later found out, he could sell the coupons on the black market. Instead of receiving the regular price of five marks from the government for the coupons, he received eighty marks on the black market.

In the barn where we slept was a beautiful machine which helped the farmer take the hay into the barn. It was the first time I had seen such a nice piece of equipment, so I asked the farmer if all German farmers were so equipped.

"No," he said. "This is not German equipment, but French."

"Did you buy it?" I asked him.

"No," he replied. "This is my war booty."

"But did you pay for it?" I questioned.

"Are you crazy!" He exclaimed. "We occupied France and whatever was there belonged to Germans. Everyone who took part in the fighting was entitled to take what he wanted. We paid for it with our blood."

"But that was morally wrong, in my opinion," I said. "You were not entitled to steal from the French."

He looked at me, gave a characteristic German "*Scheisse,*" and left the barn.

Looking around the barn, we also saw another new piece of farm equipment. We checked the inscription and found that it was a plow and grass cutter with French names. It was more of the "war booty" the farmer had taken. Of course, he had paid nothing to the French farmer from whom he had taken the equipment. The French farmer was supposed to have been happy that he was not arrested and sent to a concentration camp.

To bring such heavy equipment into the barn, it was necessary to use big trucks. This was impossible without the permission of the German authorities. This indicated that looting was accepted and even encouraged by the German administration.

After breakfast we continued our trip on foot. For lunch we stopped at another German farm. We met threee young girls who were forced laborers from eastern Europe. One was Polish and the other two were sisters from western Ukraine. The Polish girl said that she had contacted the Polish Red Cross and was waiting to go home or perhaps to England where there was a large group of Polish soldiers. The Ukrainian girls were confused and told us that they were afraid to be sent home because it was known that the Russians regarded everyone from western Ukraine as an enemy of Communism. They therefore expected to be sent to the concentration camp in Siberia. They asked us to help them.

I asked the farmer to help them hide until they had the opportunity to join a Ukrainian group. That he promised to do.

A few days later we came to a small town, Reding. Here

we met a larger group of workers from eastern Europe who were organized as a community under the protection of the UNRRA. We were asked, when we explained that we were former prisoners of the concentration camps, if we had an official certification of our being held in the concentration camps. We didn't, so we were told to go back to the concentration camp where there was an American administration and get our certification because it would be very important in the future to have such an identification card. We decided to go back, and an American soldier offered his car to take us there.

We asked him to stop at the farm where we had met the three girls. Since we knew about the existence of a camp for displaced persons where all former slave workers from eastern and central Europe were brought in and received help and protection from international organizations, we made arrangements with the American soldier who was taking us to Ebenseee to take the girls to the DP camp. However, only the Polish girl was still at the farm. She told us that almost immediately after we had left, the German farmer had gone to the police and called the Russian Committee for Repatriation to take the Ukrainian girls. When the commission had come, the girls were terrified and refused to go. With the help of the German farmer and police, the Russians took them away by force. The Polish girl explained to us that the German farmer was afraid that his behavior toward one of the girls would be revealed, since during the Nazi era, when she had to work on his farm as a slave, he had made advances to her and when she refused him, he raped her repeatedly. He was also afraid that she had become pregnant, so he seized this opportunity to rid himself of the girls, although he knew what would happen to them if they were taken by the Russian Commission. Now we were aware that not only the Germans in the concentration camps but also German farmers were less than human toward the *"auslanders"* (non-Germans) brought by force from eastern and central Europe.

We were very angry, but the American soldier guessed what was going on and prevented us from taking revenge. We could only spit in the farmer's face and then had to leave the farm.

In the concentration camp at Ebensee we found many

former prisoners from eastern Europe. They had organized an administration by national committees and were being helped by UNRRA and the International Red Cross.

We found that immediately after the capitulation, special missions came from France, Belgium, and Holland to take all the French, Belgian, and Dutch prisoners home. The problem was with the eastern European prisoners because only a few of them wanted to go back to their countries. The others preferred to remain in the free world. Each nationality formed its own committee; together they organized a general committee for all prisoners.

We also heard about a tragic misunderstanding, an error made inadvertently by the American detachment which had come to liberate the camp. Wanting to help the prisoners as soon as they could, the soldiers gave everyone a CARE package, not knowing how dangerous this was. The starved prisoners gulped down the food without any control, and many of them died as a result. There was talk that from two hundred to two thousand prisoners had died that way.

In contact with the International Red Cross and UNRRA, I organized a Ukrainian committee and found many of my friends who, until then, had pretended to be Polish, Russian, or Czech in order to escape deportation to Soviet Russia. Now all Ukrainians were brought into one block and were given plenty of food and other things we needed.

We remained there for a few weeks but, as I have mentioned before, we were anxious for information about the political situation in Ukraine. We wanted to get into contact with other Ukrainian groups, so we decided to go to Munich where we had been told there was a bigger organization.

This was not such a simple thing to do, because the division between Germany and Austria had already been established and it was necessary to get a permit to go from Austria to Germany. I decided to visit the American colonel who was the chief of administration for this section of Austria. When I came into his office, his secretary asked me to come in. When I opened the door I was surprised to see two shoes on the desk instead of an officer sitting in a chair, so I left his office thinking that perhaps the colonel was drunk. The secretary told me to go back in and smilingly explained that this was the American way to be comfortable—to sit in a chair behind a desk and prop up one's feet.

I explained our problem to the colonel. He insisted that we remain where we were. He said that we would be provided with everything we need and there was no reason for us to leave Austria. He also told us that another reason we should remain that there was temporarily a problem of transportation. But at last we were permitted to enter Bavaria. The whole group of Ukrainians who had been in Ebensee was thus transferred to Munich.

There we found a large Ukrainian community consisting of more than ten thousand refugees. They were located, along with refugees of other countries of eastern Europe (Poland, Latvia, Lithuania, Estonia, etc.), in three big groups for displaced persons on the outskirts of Munich. Many Ukrainians lived inside Munich away from the camps. We also met a group of former Ukrainian political prisoners from Dachau, Saxenhausen, Buchenwald, and other concentration camps who had been liberated by American or English soldiers in April. They had met in Munich and had organized a committee of Ukrainian victims of Nazi persecution. Former political prisoners who had decided to remain in Germany under the protection of the UNRRA were asked to go to the UNRRA camp with all other displaced persons. They were promised help from this organization. Psychologically, however, this was unacceptable because the crowded conditions of the camp recalled the concentration camps. Everyone who had just escaped from such a life preferred to remain in a room in the city, although by so doing, all rights to help and food were forfeited. The Ukrainian group of former prisoners had a hotel room from the German administration. There was enough room, but the problem was food and clothing, and soon there was the additional problem of heating because of the approach of fall and winter.

We soon found out that even now, free and under the protection of the American army, we were in an inconvenient situation. Former German political prisoners had organized a committee—"KZ *Betreuungsstelle*"—for taking care of those persons, providing them with food, food coupons, and all other things they needed. When I came to them as a representative of the Ukrainian group and asked for their support, I was told that this organization was *"nur für Deutsche"* ("for Germans only"), so the slogan *"nur für Deutsche"* so well known during the war in all occupied countries had been revived and applied again in "KZ *Betreuungstelle."* We were refused any help because we were not German. Then we asked the administration that we be given help on the grounds that we were private persons living in Germany, but they, too, refused, saying that prisoners did not belong to them, but only to the *"Betreuungsstelle."* It was not an easy problem to solve, because in both cases there were extremely long lines of people waiting and it took many hours before one had a chance to explain the reason for coming.

When I visited the *"Betreuungsstelle"* for the second time, I asked the officer to give me a written declaration that this committee was only for taking care of German former prisoners. He complied. Until today I have a written document that former German prisoners of the concentration camps liked the idea expressed in the slogan *"nur für deutsche"* and even in those hard times when there was a shortage of everything, they refused to help non-German victims of the Nazi persecution.

With this statement in hand, I returned to the office where the coupons for buying food and clothing were issued and again was refused what we needed. A German waiting his turn suggested that I go to another clerk and tell him privately that we were a group of Germans who had been American prisoners of war who had just arrived. I did as he suggested and was immediately supplied with our needs.

It took many trips to the many different offices of the German administration, American occupation, and the DP camps before finally the German administration of Munich accepted the fact that we would live privately and would receive coupons as the rest of the population of Germany.

The owner of the hotel where we lived fled Munich during the last days of the fighting. Soon he returned and although he had been a member of the Nazi party, when he applied for the hotel he was granted his request. So, on order of the administration, we were transferred to a big school building on the other side of Munich called Ramersdorf. All schools had been closed immediately after the war, so the buildings were empty. There was plenty of room here, but there was a need for furniture other than that found in the school and there was no way for us to take baths. Soon the three-tiered bunks were brought from Dachau concentration camp so we had a place to sleep.

Soon winter came, much earlier and colder than usual. There was already a shortage in heating material, so now there was a real problem. After the portion we had been given for heating the building was gone, I went to the mayor of Munich and asked him for additional coal or wood. Herr Wimmer, the mayor, was chatting with another man. They had no business to discuss; it was just a friendly conversation. When I mentioned that I was representing the Ukrainian group in the school building, the other gentlemen came into the conversation and said, "Oh, Ukrainian. Then you are an SS. Were you a guard in the concentration camp?" I told Herr Wimmer that this was insulting and asked who the man was. He told me that he was a friend of his who had been imprisoned in a concentration camp himself as a member of the German Socialist Democratic party. I asked him in what camp he had been imprisoned, and he told me Melk. I asked Herr Wimmer to tell me his name because I recognized him as a *blockältester* in Melk. He had been known as one who liked to torture non-German political prisoners. I wanted to bring him to responsibility immediately for his previous conduct. The man jumped up, took his hat, and began to leave. I asked Herr Wimmer to stop him and call the police. I said I would bring other witnesses who would testify that this man was a sadist and should not be in the administration of Democratic Germany, but should be brought to court for what he had done. Herr Wimmer told me that this was all some kind of misunderstanding and that I should tell him what I had come for. In the meantime his friend quickly disappeared.

I explained our problem and asked him to help us with coal or wood. He said that there was a general shortage, but he had a good idea. He told me that there was a forest not far from Munich from which the wood was brought. Since it was very cold, the former Nazis who had been obliged to work there refused to go to work, saying that it was too cold. He suggested that we go to the forest and cut the wood; two-thirds of what we cut would go to the city and one-third would be ours. I brought to his attention that he had declared that he had always been anti-Nazi and should think of the humanitarian point of view. I said the former Nazis who had never lacked for food or clothing during the war and were now in very good physical condition and lived comfortably could not go to work because it was too cold. Yet we, who had just survived by a miracle and were not yet in very good health and had problems obtaining clothing and shoes, were supposed to be able to go to work and get wood for others as well as ourselves. Even though the Nazi administration was over, we still would have to work like slaves while the Nazis sat in a warm room and waited for the wood we cut to be brought to them. He was shocked by the implications of what I had told him. He said that he only wanted to attack the problem from a practical point of view and it seemed to him to be the simplest solution. He said that he had not seen it as I had but, nonetheless, it was the only solution at present. We had nothing to do but accept, so for the next three days we cut trees in the extreme cold. One-third of what we cut was brought to the school building.

In political and psychological respects, it was an extremely interesting illustration of what the Germans really were. The new *oberburgermeister* of Munich, a member of the Socialist Party, who had declared himself an arch-enemy of National Socialism, continued to regard non-German people as something inferior. For him, even the Nazi leaders from the war were worth more than their victims.

The same attitude we met wherever we came to the offices of the new German administration. Most shocking of all was that KZ *Betreuungstelle*, for former victims of Nazi persecution, continued the policy of *"nur für Deutsche"* and refused to help any non-Germans. This was soon relaxed in the case of the Polish and Yugoslavian prisoners because the Poles found among the exiles a Polish colonel and he, assisted by a colonel from the American army, asked the KZ *Betreuungsstelle* why they refused to help the Poles. The German officer explained that this was just a misunderstanding; they always wanted to do what was possible for them. The same thing happened in the case of the Yugoslavian former prisoners. However, they continued to refuse the Ukrainians and since the Ukrainians had no exile army and the Ukraine was occupied by Russia and all Ukrainians were supposed to be arrested and sent to Russia for repatriation, none of the former German political prisoners wanted to support us in our requests that we be treated like other victims of the persecution.

When an administration in the part of Germany under French, English, and American occupation was established, the problem of support for the victims of the Nazis became an important one to the new administration. Offices were established in the larger cities for taking care of the victims of Nazi persecution, and compensation for all victims, without regard to race, nationality, or any other consideration, was promised. Even then, discrimination against the Ukrainians continued. This was because the main force in the offices was German Communist—those under the supervision of Russian emissaries. Russian Communists who occupied Ukraine were trying to get all Ukrainians who were abroad for repatriation. Those who refused to return were persecuted. Therefore, the German Communists, knowing tnat they were pleasing the Russians in East Germany, stubbornly continued their refusal to give the Ukrainians any help.

Soon a special secretary in the new German government was established with responsibility for caring for the former victims of the Nazi persecution. An office called the *Staatskommisariat fur Politisch Verfolgte* (State Commissary for Victims of Political Persecution) was established in Munich. I knew the secretary in this office was Dr. Auerbach, a German Jew. Since he himself had been a victim of the persecution and had been in Auschwitz, we expected that his treatment of us would be different. We were disappointed, however, for he told us that he was not interested in interfering with the Germans and had no intention of changing their decision.

The fighting for our group took almost three years. Finally, a German newspaper agreed to publish an article I had written accusing not only the Germans of continuing their hatred of non-Germans, but also attacking Auerbach for changing the Nazi ideal of Germans on the top and Jews on the bottom to Jews on the top and Ukrainians on the bottom.

There was no one who wanted to fight for the Ukrainians, I insisted, because the USSR, an important political power, was interested in persecuting us. In answer, Auerbach gave his excuses in the newspaper. I returned my answer. A few days later Auerbach invited me for a personal interview. We discussed the problem and finally he agreed that we were truly entitled to the same rights as all the others. He organized a committee consisting of three persons to check all Ukrainians and verify their documents. The committee was headed by me because he knew me personally from Auschwitz. Also, I gave him witnesses from Auschwitz, some German Democratic Socialists, and even a Dutch Communist, who had known me there as a political prisoner.

Thus, after three years of the new political administration, we were at last acknowledged as having the same right to help and compensation as victims from other nations.

Chapter 25

"WIEDERGUTMACHUNG": UNFULFILLED PROMISES AND OBLIGATIONS

On September 19, 1945, the U.S. Military Command in occupied Germany issued Proclamation No. 2, in which a just compensation was promised to all victims of Nazi persecution. This promise was repeated in Proclamation No. 4, on March 1, 1947. And on February 6, 1950, the U.S. High Commisioner, J. McCloy, in his public speech in Stuttgart, Germany, declared:

> It is the U.S.A.'s demand that all persons who suffered under Nazi terror because of race or political reasons receive a just compensation. Their sufferings can never be totally compensated. Nevertheless, the problem of just compensation to these people must be considered with utmost seriousness. A rehabilitation of Germany without regard to this problem would be wrong and would be an omen of future calamities.

The appearance of thousands of living skeletons freed by American and English armies from German concentration camps, and the discovery of the horrors applied by the Nazis in those "Mills of Death," resulting in the brutal annihilation of about nine million victims, horrified even the German population. They feared revenge or at least severe punishment for these horrible crimes. Therefore, the obligation of a just compensation for all the victims of Nazi persecution was accepted by all Germans without any protest. In June, 1946, the Bavarian Prime Minister, Dr. Hoegner, proclaimed an obligation to compensate all non-German victims of Nazi persecution a "commandmant of the national honor of the German nation" (*"Ehrenpflicht des deutschen Volkes"*).

As soon as a new German administration was organized in Western Germany, a special office for compensation, called the *Wiedergutmachungsamt*, was added at each level. At the top level, a *ministerium* for compensation affairs in each *land* was created. These offices started to support the victims of Nazi persecution who survived imprisonment in the concentration camps with the first doses of compensation. The final decision in each individual case, however, had to come according to the regulations of a special claim law, which was yet to be passed by the German authorities.

Had the victims of Nazi persecution then pressed for a quick solution, the problem would have been solved.

But the former prisoners of the concentration camps didn't press. On the contrary, they supported a slowdown in the procedure. The reason was the German currency of the time. Destruction of the "Third Reich" brought an immediate and striking inflation. The difference between the nominal and the real value of the Reichsmark was 1:200. Officially, everything was regulated by coupons distributed each month to each individual. However, if a pound of butter cost one Reichsmark on the coupon, on the black market it cost 200 Reichsmark. If compensation would have been paid in such a situation, it would have been a mockery of a real compensation. Because of the existing severe limitations on everything through coupons, one would have been forced to spend one's compensation, the cash, on the black market, and there receive for a "fortune" of, say, ten thousand Reichsmark, fifty pounds of butter! Therefore, it was necessary to wait until a devaluation of German currency.

Finally, in June, 1948 came the widely known "D Day": a devaluation and replacement of the Reichsmark, RM, by the new German currency, the Deutsche Mark, DM. Since the stabilization of the new German currency in Western Germany was heavily supported by billions of U.S. dollars, the DM became—and remains today—the most stable currency in the world.

Now was the right time to demand the payment of the promised compensation, the more so that West·Germany immediately after "D Day" proved to be a rich country. While, until "D Day," it was extremely hard to buy anything even with coupons, almost overnight there appeared a plentiful supply of everything. The stores became full of all types of merchandise.

We knew the secret of the "miracle." At the start of the war, Nazi Germany stockpiled a reserve supply for four years for Germany's population, in order to meet the anticipated severe embargo. But, as a result of the occupation by Germany of almost all Europe, these reserves were not only not used, but were enlarged by the systematic contributions from occupied territories. Additionally, every one of the millions of Germans who was in occupied territory as a soldier or member of the German administration, established his own reserves. They looted as *kriegsbeute* (war booty) whatever they could and sent it home. So all the cellars in West Germany were overloaded. In East Germany the Russian administration carefully checked each room, each cellar, and confiscated everything. In West Germany, neither the Americans nor the English touched any part of these rich storages.

It didn't pay to sell anything for the inflated Reichsmark. But it did pay, for the strong D-mark. So when, on the eve of "D-Day," the issuing of a strong D-mark was proclaimed, overnight the stored goods were brought to stores, to shops, and into closets and kitchens. Thus, overnight the severe shortage was "miraculously" replaced by an abundance of everything.

Seeing all this, we hoped that during the next month there would be no problem receiving the promised compensation.

Unfortunately, this was not to be. The "cold war" between the United States and Russia strongly changed the psychological and political attitudes of West Germans. In their opinion, Germany had become a very important factor in the "cold war." So their fear and submission disappeared, and the notorious German arrogance reappeared. In addition, as the *Encyclopedia Americana* states,

Denazification . . . proved to be a complete failure. By the early 1950's practically all former members of the Nazi party had regained their standing and had infiltrated, on a wide front, into governmental, administrative, judicial and academic careers.

Therefore, the projected Claims Law, as prepared by the German authorities, provided compensation only for German victims of Nazi persecution, totally excluding all non-German victims. Fortunately, any new German law at that time needed the official approval of the U.S. High Commisioner for Germany. McCloy, the High Commisioner, refused to approve such a discriminatory law and firmly demanded the inclusion of all non-German victims of Nazi persecution as well. When the Germans learned how strong the influence of Jews is in the United States, they agreed to include the surviving Jewish victims in the Claims Law. This was underscored when it was clearly indicated that the restitution of German capital in the United States, confiscated during the war, and a special financial subsidy for West Germany, depended on Germany's actual payment of compensation to Jewish victims of Nazi persecution. However, Germany adamantly refused to pay compensation to all others—non-German and non-Jewish victims.

But U.S. High Commisioner McCloy insisted and finally in the fall of 1949 a compromise was reached. The "First Claims Law" was passed, providing a "just compensation" to all, including non-German and non-Jewish victims of Nazi persecution.

Unfortunately, it very soon became evident that the Germans had only trickery in mind. First, the realization of the provided-for-by-law compensation was purposely slowed down by an extremely complicated procedure, a super-red tape; everyone who applied for compensation was required to produce all kinds of certifications—personal, medical, in regard to the time and place of imprisonment, the reason for imprisonment, personal declarations, attestations of three witnesses, etc.

When all of these had been submitted, then every application of non-German and non-Jewish victims was turned down. Paying of compensation had been refused. The motivation was: the law provides a compensation for any victim "who was persecuted in Nazi prisons and concentration camps due to political activity, race, religion or world philosophy" (*weltanscanung*). None of these reasons could be applied to the non-German and non-Jewish victims. These, Ukrainain, Polish, and other so-called displaced persons, the German authorities declared, were put into concentration camps because of their nationality. The issued Claims Law provides no compensation for such a category. The German authorities didn't even hide their sharing of the opinion that the German people committed no crimes whatsoever relating to any non-German during World War II and therefore refused to pay any compensation to any non-German former prisoners of German concentration camps. This was not Hitler's war, they insisted, but a war by the entire German nation in the interest of all the German people, a war absolutely right and just in moral, political, and legal aspirations. The people of all the countries occupied by Germany, they insisted, were obligated to obey the German authorities, and when one refused and rebelled, he had to be, legally and justly, imprisoned or even executed.

This opinion was expressed quite frankly and boldly in private conversations by all Germans, and even in decisions refusing compensation to non-German victims. So, for instance, in the case of a Polish former prisoner, Dr. Niedsielski, the negative decision concerning his right to receive a compensation according to the Claims Law as one who was persecuted by the Nazis because of his political activity against Nazism officially stated:

If the applicant expects that the Term "political activity against Nazism" used in the Claims Law includes the opposition of non-Germans to the Third Reich's foreign policy as well, he is wrong. A changing of the political conditions imposed on the German nation by the Versailles peace treaty was a necessity and duty of the entire German nation since a German signature was forced onto this treaty. The action in this respect was not started first by the National-Socialistic government of Germany.

In the case of the Polish victim, Trojnarski, the German appeals court in Detmold in its negative decision declared:

There is no doubt that the concentration camps were created by the Nazi government for the persecution of victims because of their political activity, race, religion, or philosophy, as it is defined in the Claims Law. However, during the war these camps were also used for the confinement of those citizens of German occupied countries who resisted the German authorities, and this is perfectly consistent with the international law and with justice. In this respect, concentration camps were in no way created first by the national socialistic Third Reich. There were, for instance, the English concentration camps in South Africa during the Anglo-Boer war.

The office responsible for compensations in Hannover in its negative decision in the case of K. Grusczynski, on June 13, 1949, went still further:

Since Mr. Gruszczynski had been held in a concentration camp not because of political, but because of a national-Polish-political [sic!] reason, it should be investigated why he was not executed, nor put in a prisoners of war camp, but in a concentration camp.

Working as a representative and lawyer for Ukrainian victims of Nazi persecution, I was confronted every day with such a wanton interpretation of the compensation law by all German officers and with their arrogance and hatred toward all *ausländers*, i.e., foreigners.

This occurred not only in problems of compensation, but everywhere. Thus, for instance, I was badly treated in problems of obtaining an apartment and merchandise. Because of a housing shortage, one could find an apartment or even a room only through a permit of the official housing office. Being single, in 1945, I received only one room, sharing an apartment of four rooms, one kitchen, and one toilet with three other German families. In 1946, I married and applied for another room—unsuccessfully. In 1948, my first son was born. My mother-in-law, a refugee, came to assist my wife, and I applied for an apartment. In vain. In 1950, a second son was born. I sent new applications and letters to all types of offices, but all in vain. One day, one room of the apartment I lived in became vacant, so I applied for it immediately. But the family—Drippel—living in another room of the apartment, applied for Mrs. Drippel's stepmother. The family had no children, and there was absolutely no need for bringing their stepmother from the village she lived to Munich. Nevertheless, the housing authority gave the room not to my family, but to the stepmother of Mrs. Drippel, because she was a German and the widow of a prominent Nazi. So the German family—consisting of three persons—received two rooms, and my family—consisting of three adults and two children—received only one room in the same apartment. When my protest came to the state secretary for housing and an investigation was ordered, the responsible officers declared that it was merely a misunderstanding. They believed that since I had a doctorate degree, I must be a physician and they were still looking—for five years!—for an apartment for my family. Of course, the mistake would be rectified in a few days and my family would receive at least two rooms. However, until my emigration to the United States in January, 1952, my family of five persons had to live in one room in Munich, where hundreds of families of formerly prominent Nazis, consisting of three or even two persons, were given three-room apartments.

The same occurred with the coupons used for buying any merchandise. I was given a very hard time before I received a coupon for some clothing for myself and my family once a month. But the German family living in the same apartment received coupons easily each week, even though in 1952 they still had four big coffers full of French and Polish garments, stockings, and fabrics. They used to sell their coupons to me at the black market prices.

Of course, all non-German victims of Nazi persecution vehemently protested against this new persecution by a democratic Germany. A committee consisting of representatives of Ukrainian, Polish, and Yugoslavian former prisoners of Nazi concentration camps took any opportunity to send protests and memorandums to the German authorities; to the governments of West Germany, the United States, Great Britain, and France; to the U.N., U.N.R.R.A., I.R.O.; to American, English, and French senators and politicians; and to the American, English, and French press.

"You must be patient until the final decision is made by the German authorities," the U.S. High Commissioner suggested. So we were. Of course, it took time until the higher, and then the highest, German court issued decisions definitively denying the promised compensation to non-German and non-Jewish victims.

Then, under pressure, West Germany replaced all previous compensation laws, issued by *lands*, by a new federal law. This was passed on June 29, 1956 under the title, "The Federal Claims Law" (*Bundesentschadigunsgesetz*, the *BEG*). The text of the new law essentially was almost identical to the previous claims laws. But it was accompanied by official promises that now, according to the new law, there would be absolutely no discrimination and all former prisoners of the Nazi concentration camps from Eastern Europe, now political refugees called "DPs" (displaced persons), would soon receive the same compensation as did the German and Jewish victims of Nazi persecution.

We didn't any more trust the "new democratic" Germany and demanded that the execution of the compensation to the "DP" be transferred to an international organization, say a special section of the U.N., I.R.O., the International Red Cross, or something similar. We brought to attention the very basic principle of the jurisdiction: *"Nemo judex in causa sua,"* i.e., no one may serve as the judge in his own case. How can a German make an important decision concerning German guilt and Germany's obligation to compensate a Ukrainian or

Polish victim of German persecution? In these cases Germany as a nation was accused. This was clearly stated on each application: "The case . . . against the Federal Republic of Germany" and every German was legally and morally a part of the German nation.

Unfortunately, our demand expressed in our memorandums to the governments of the United States, Great Britain, and France, and to the U.N. and other international organizations, was ignored. We were told that we must trust the new Germany since it wasn't Nazi anymore, but truly democratic.

It didn't take long to see that we were absolutely right in our mistrust toward the "new democratic" Germany. Had there been true good will on the side of the German authorities to fairly and honestly compensate all non-German and non-Jewish victims of Nazi persecutions as well, the responsible German offices would now have simply changed, in each case, the previous negative decision to a positive one. Since all requested documents were already, in each case, added to the previous application, and proved, there would be no problem to complete the procedure in merely a few months. Instead, the German authorities restarted the procedure from the very beginning, requesting in each case new applications, new declarations, new documents, new statements of three witnesses. They demanded even original birth certification, even though everyone knew that these applicants, as political refugees, could not correspond with the Russian government occupying their country. Then the German authorities started to turn down all applications as before. The Ukrainian, Polish, and Yugoslavian prisoners of Nazi concentration camps, they insisted, were persecuted not because of their political activity, race, or religion, but because of their nationality and therefore, according to the new Claims Law, were not entitled to any compensation.

In May, 1957, I went to West Germany in order to bring my case as a precedent to the special compensation court. Before my emmigration to the United States I worked as a lawyer. Therefore I was permitted to act now, as a lawyer, in my own case.

The chairman of the new Bavarian court for compensation, called *entschädigungskammer*, was Dr. Jagomast, the same one who was in that position under the previous claims law. I knew him very well, since, until 1952, while representing all Ukrainian cases, I met him almost daily. Dr. Jagomast was a very talkative person. Now, in May, 1957, when I met him again, he greeted me sarcastically, "I'm glad to see you again, Dr. Mirchuk. But frankly, I don't understand why you are losing your money by coming to Munich. Are you already an American millionaire?"

"On the contrary, Dr. Jagomast," I answered, "I am as poor as a church mouse and came here to receive my compensation for my four years of slave work and for the brutal torturing I received in the German concentration camps."

"Sir," Dr. Jagomast said slowly, underlining each word, "I told you many times before and I will tell you once more— Ukrainian former prisoners of German concentration camps will receive no compensation. Not one penny."

"But Germany officially, morally, and legally took over an obligation to give all non-German victims of Nazi persecution a just compensation equal to what the German and Jewish people received."

"This humiliating obligation was forced upon us, as was the Versailles peace treaty. We refuse to carry it out since West Germany is now a free nation."

"But the Bavarian Prime Minister, Dr. Hoegner, called the honest realization of that obligation a 'commandment' on the honor of the German nation."

"Baloney! He had to say so in that situation for propaganda purposes. But he himself didn't mean that. On the contrary, we are adamant concerning the principle that during World War II, Germany committed no crimes, no injustices to foreigners and, therefore, there is no reason whatsoever to pay any compensation."

"Dr. Jagomast," I remarked, "the condemnation law talks of compensation to victims of *Nazi* persecution. Don't you see and take into account the difference between the Nazi regime and Germany?"

"No," he insisted firmly. "Because there was not and there is not any such difference. Hitler was elected by a majority of the German nation legally and democratically. His government was supported by at least eighty percent of all Germany to the very last. The war was not Hitler's but Germany's—desired and conducted by the entire German nation."

"And what about the atrocities and horrible crimes committed on millions of victims in German concentration camps?"

"That is propaganda! A *greuelpropaganda*! We are sick and tired of that. We refuse to accept that any more!"

"But I hope that you will be compelled to respect your legal, international obligation to compensate justly all non-German victims."

"Compelled!" Dr. Jagomast said sarcastically. "By whom? And for whom? For a handful of refugees who have no support in their own country nor anywhere else from anyone else?"

These extremely frank declarations of Dr. Jagomast, the chairman of the new Bavarian *entschädigungkammer*, were in no way encouraging. But I decided to go through to the end. In addition to the previous documents supporting the right of Ukrainian former prisoners of Nazi concentration camps, I now brought a lenghty *gutachten*, the opinion of Dr. F. Boehm, an outstanding law professor at a German university and a member of the West German parliament (*Bundestag*), who was co-author of the latest Federal Indemnification Law, the *BEG*. Possessing great skill and deep knowledge of both the law and of the problem of Ukrainian victims, Dr. Boehm, in his almost ten-thousand-word opinion, examined the subject in great detail. He concluded that there can be no doubt that the Ukrainians, former prisoners of Nazi concentration camps, were persecuted because of: 1. their political activity against the Nazis; 2. their philosphy, which was contrary to Hitlerite ideology; and 3. their nationality. Therefore, they are entitled to complete compensation as provided by the Federal Indemnification Law.

Two witnesses gave important written declarations, Professor Erich von Mende, former deputy to Hitler's Secretary of State Rosenberg, testified that he heard many conversations between Himmler and Kaltenbrunner, Himmler's deputy, describing the members of the Ukrainian underground movement, O.U.N. as political and ideological arch-enemies of the German Nazis. Another witness, Dr. Peter Schenk, the former chief of Hitler's *SD* in Lvov, testified that he heard the same many times from the German governor and from the chief of the Gestapo in Western Ukraine.

Dr. Jagomast accepted these documents with an ironic remark: "That's all *für die Katzen*—good for nothing!"

During the first session of the trial, Dr. Jagomast asked me, "You mentioned your discussion with the first governor of Galicia in Lvov, Dr. Lasch, before your arrest in 1941. Do you know where he is now?"

"As far as I know, he was killed during the war. But if it is important, you may ask Professor Hans Koch, who worked with him and now resides here in Munich."

"Yes, it is important. I will ask Professor Koch. Therefore, the trial is adjourned for one month."

"Why for one month?" I asked. "Professor Koch is in his office two blocks from here. You can call him and he will be here in one hour."

"I have made my decision," Dr. Jagomast delcared with theatrical seriousness. "So, *auf wiedersehen*, I will see you again in one month."

He did the same regarding the testimony of witnesses Professor von Mende and Dr. Schenk, then with Prof. Boehm, and also for four other "reasons." The trial was adjourned seven times and took seven months, instead of being held and concluded in one day. Then, finally came the decision:

In the name of the [German] nation—*abgelehnt*—my decision is negative. Ukrainians, members of O.U.N., were held in German prisons and concentration camps neither by reason of their political convictions, race, or religion, nor of their political opposition to Naziism, but because of their nationality and, accordingly, are not entitled to any compensation as provided by the Federal Indemnation Law.

After the Trial I asked Dr. Jagomast, "So you declared on behalf of the German nation that the Ukrainian victims had been imprisoned by the German authorities because of their nationality. Does this mean that you officially accept the *collectiveschuld*, the responsibility of the entire German nation for what was done by the Gestapo in occupied territories?"

"Jawohl," he answered. "Yes, sir. With only one correction: we Germans committed no crimes to any foreigners during World War II."

I appealed to the *entschädigungsenat*, the higher indemnation court. But my appeal was turned down. And the *bundesgerichtshof*, the supreme court of West Germany, refused even to review the case, which was to be a precedent for twelve hundred Ukrainian victims of Nazi persecution, who had survived.

In my dealings with members of the German courts and other authorities relating to compensations, I was puzzled by their consistent use of "we." "We" was who? The answer to this question I found first in T. H. Tetens book *The New Germany and the Old Nazis*:

> Major General Hans Korte describes how a kind of General Staff, or "screening committee" was set up in Munich to direct all the anti-war guilt propaganda in occupied Germany and throughout the entire world. A group of Nazi jurists who had served in Nuremberg as counsels for the major war criminals formed the nucleus of the directing body. Prominent among them were Dr. Rudolf Aschenauer of Munich and Ernst Achnenback of Essen.

So, after twelve years following the capitulation of Hitler's Third Reich and after three indemnification laws had been issued by the democratic West German Republic, the situation hadn't changed. It was as pictured by Terence Pirtee in her *Germany*: "There are hundreds of ex-Nazis drawing fat pensions, while thousands of victims of Nazism have had to fight for the barest restitution."

On behalf of twelve hundred Ukrainians, former political prisoners of the German concentration camps, I asked the chancellor of West Germany for an audience to discuss the problem of the officially promised, but until today unfulfilled, compensation to these victims of Nazi persecution. He refused, and asked me to send him a written report. I did. Soon, I received, from the chancellor's secretary, an answer dated June 14, 1958, which concluded, " . . . Federal Republic of Germany . . . passed laws and regulations providing compensation to the non-German victims equal to the one provided for German victims. So the F.D.R. totally fulfilled its obligation."

Not one of the twelve hundred Ukranian victims received the promised compensation. Instead, they found only twelve years of moral torture, with promises and requests to present applications, documents, certifications, proofs, etc., etc. Yet, "The Federal Republic of Germany totally fulfilled its oblibations." What sham!

Then the routine began once more: protests, a flood of memorandums, and lobbying. In the same situation were the Polish and Yugoslavian victims. Therefore, they did the same. Supporting us were the NCWC and the U.N. High Commissioner for refugees. I myself was twice invited to orally present our case to a special commission of the German parliament, *Bundestag*, in Bonn.

In October, 1960 an agreement was concluded between the Federal Government of West Germany and the U.N. High Commissioner for Refugees concerning "additional payments" to victims of Nazi persecution due to their nationality. These "additional payments," according to the agreement, included not one penny for the slave work done in the concentration camps, not one penny in restitution for what was confiscated by the Gestapo during arrest, not one penny for losses incurred through separation from professional work, and not one penny for widows and children of the murdered or diseased victims. All of these compensations and benefits provided by the BEG and realized for all German and Jewish victims were flatly and totally denied by the new agreement regarding "nationality" victims. The only benefits provided by the agreement were disability payments equal to the percentage of damage caused by persecution to the victim's health and ability to work. Actually, this was not an indemnification, but a payment provided to all workers by the existing German social security laws and regulations. Since we, as prisoners of the German concentration camps, did work there, in Germany and for Germany, the German government being our employer, we were all legally entitled to such payments. But even this had been denied us. Now, acknowledging this, the Germans, for propaganda purposes, of course, preferred to call them "additional payments to nationality victims."

And now, for the fourth time, everything started from the very beginning: new applications, new documents, attests, etc. The result was that a handful of applicants were granted a rent, but about ninety percent were denied even that, because they were "persecuted not because of their nationality, but because of the requirements of military or police security." Our new protest was answered by the Federal Finance Minister on October 19, 1962, exactly as it was on June 14, 1958: "The Federal Government of Germany fulfilled all its indemnification obligations fairly, totally and definitively."

During my conference in the finance ministerium, I had some very interesting exchanges of opinion. "There shouldn't be any more complaints," I was told. "West Germany paid more than seven billion dollars of indemnification to foreigners, victims of Nazi persecution. Can you imagine—seven billion!"

"You are talking of compensation to Jewish victims," I answered, "therefore let me bring to your attention what they say. First, these billions, and more, you received from the United States. What you really did was to put the American subsidy into German industry and then forward the 'indemnification' in the form of industrial products to the Jewish victims. Secondly, even if you had paid it all with your own money, the amount would be less than ten percent of what Nazi Germany took from six million Jewish victims. However, I am neither entitled nor competent to discuss the Jewish-German problems with you. I represent Ukrainian victims of Nazi persecution. Why do you refuse to compensate them?"

"And why should we? What for? We have no money!"

"Sir," I remarked, "according to reports in the German press during the war, Germans brought, every day, long freight trains loaded with corn, meat, butter, and all types of merchandise worth millions of dollars, from Ukraine. This lasted three years and gained billions of dollars. Germany paid not one penny for all of this. In addition, over three million Ukrainians worked as slaves in Germany and for Germany for over three years, and were paid practically nothing.

This adds more billions of dollars to the total that Germany owes Ukrainians. If you paid only the interest on what you owe, this would be sufficient to pay a just compensation to Ukrainian victims."

My interlocutor suddenly developed problems with his throat and excused himself to get some water. When he returned, I continued. "In addition, *Herr Doctor*, three million German soldiers in occupied Ukraine for three years privately looted food and other items and sent them to their families in Germany, paying not one penny for all this."

Herr Doctor again developed problems with his throat.

The promised just indemnification, so loudly and solemnly proclaimed many times, has not been granted to Ukrainian former prisoners of the German "Mills of Death" even to the present day.

EPILOGUE

I began my memoirs about my four-year experience in the German "Mills of Death", where I served as a political prisoner from 1941 to 1945, by noting that I am a Ukrainian, and by briefly explaining why Ukrainians came to be prisoners of the Nazi concentration camps. Today, with the reprinting of my memoirs, I think it necessary to say a little more on this theme in my "Epilogue". For the post-war situation evolved in such a way that even today the Western world is amazed that a Ukrainian was a political prisoner of the Nazi concentration camps, destined for destruction, and that he was not the only Ukrainian there, but one of thousands of Ukrainians.

The reason for this is as follows. When, after the fall of Hitler's Germany, the states of Central and Western Europe which had been occupied during the Second World War were liberated, the Ukraine found itself under the direct occupation of Soviet Russia. By its very political and moral essence the new occupant proved to be the twin brother of Nazi Germany, particularly in relation to the Ukraine and the Ukrainians. The liberation struggle of the Ukrainian people, directed against the Nazis at the time of the German occupation, was now directed against Soviet Russia. Because Moscow had recognized Ukrainian nationalists, uncompromising Ukrainian freedom fighters, as its most dangerous enemy, it has conducted from the very beginning of the new occupation of Ukraine a fierce struggle against Ukrainian nationalists. In this struggle Moscow pays special attention to the moral and political defamation of Ukrainian nationalists in the opinion of the Western world in an attempt to deprive Ukrainian nationalists, fighting for the liberation of the Ukraine from the Russian colonial yoke, of any kind of assistance from the Free World, be it material aid or political support. The aim of this dreadful defamation campaign is to portray Ukrainian nationalists who fought against the Nazis, for which they suffered and died in Nazi concentration camps, as Nazi collaborators who allegedly assisted the Germans in exterminating Jews. For this despicable task Moscow has mobilized all its agents and collaborators throughout the Free World. And yet the KGB's work has found surprisingly fertile soil among the general population of Western countries, especially the USA. On the whole the people in the West are poorly-informed about the problems of Eastern Europe. In the USA, the KGB's anti-Ukrainian propaganda has recently reached frightening proportions. This very fact compels me, in the "Epilogue" to the second edition of my memoirs, not only to say that I am Ukrainian and that the German concentration camps were filled with thousands of political prisoners like myself, but also to add a few words in order to explain who the Ukrainians are, why they were imprisoned and exterminated in the Nazi concentration camps, and how many of us there were.

*

The great French philosopher, historian and writer, Voltaire who visited the Russian Empire on the invitation of the Empress Catherine and became interested in the Cossacks and the history of the Ukrainian people, said in his account that Ukrainians have always fought for their independence. They defended their freedom against the Asiatic nomads when they had their own mighty state known as Kievan Rus'; they fought for the restoration of freedom when the Mongol hordes destroyed this state; later they fought for their freedom against the Polish invaders when Poland seized the Ukraine; and then against Muscovy which subjugated the

Ukraine and set about turning the freedom-loving Ukrainians into its slaves.

When Tsarist Russia collapsed in 1917, the Ukrainians formed their own government and proclaimed the restoration of their own independent state, the Ukrainian National Republic, on January 22, 1918. A year later, on January 22, 1919, they proclaimed the re-unification of all the Ukrainian territories into a single state.

But after several years of fierce fighting against the invading Bolshevik, White Russian and Polish armies, the Ukrainian nation became subjugated once again. The Eastern and Central regions of the Ukraine found themselves in the latest prison of nations, known as the USSR; the Western territories of the Ukraine came under Polish occupation; Bukovina was seized by Rumania; and Transcarpathian Ukraine became part of the Czechoslovakian republic.

The Ukrainian people suffered the most terrible plight under Soviet Russian occupation. The Russians destroyed the Ukrainian Church, and murdered thousands of Ukrainian priests along with their bishops and metropolitans. They also murdered hundreds of Ukrainian intellectuals, writers, poets, and cultural activists. In 1932-1933, Moscow carried out an incredibly cruel genocide. In that period not less than 7 million Ukrainian peasants were starved to death by an artificial famine.

Under Polish occupation Ukrainians lived somewhat more freely in comparison with those who lived in territories occupied by the Russians. But even under Polish rule Ukrainians were persecuted and humiliated with the aim of complete denationalization.

In such circumstances the Second World War presented the only means of escape for Ukrainians. Since Germany was fighting against both Poland and Russia, the Ukrainians, naturally, set their hopes on this conflict.

Today, from surviving Nazi documents, we know that Hitler regarded the Ukraine as the wealthy dreamland of German colonization. Thus, during the war, all Ukrainian resistance forces were to be completely destroyed and the human resources exploited for the reconstruction of war-torn

Germany. After that, the entire Ukrainian population was to be resettled in Siberia. Depopulated Ukraine was then to become the *lebensraum* of the German *uebermensch*.

But the Ukrainians were not prepared to surrender quietly to Nazi German oppression. The Nazi leadership carefully concealed its intentions, but in spite of this, the Ukrainians, nevertheless, managed to discover some of their plans. Therefore, as soon as the German army entered Ukraine, the Organization of Ukrainian Nationalists under the leadership of Stepan Bandera, the OUN-B, which led the liberation struggle of the Ukrainian nation, declared very clearly that the master of the Ukraine was the Ukrainian nation which wants to live freely in its own independent state. Later, on June 30, 1941, the Restoration of the Ukrainian State was proclaimed in Lvov, and a Ukrainian government, under the leadership of Jaroslav Stetsko, was called into being.

Once this news reached Hitler, he became furious. As a result, he ordered the Gestapo and the special units of the SD to destroy Ukrainian nationalists, "Banderites", without mercy. The members of the Ukrainian government were arrested by the Gestapo. In September, 1941, mass arrests were carried out in the parts of the Ukraine occupied by the Germans. In consequence, thousands of OUN members were sent to German prisons and concentration camps.

As the German occupation of the Ukraine continued, the Nazis divided up Ukraine's territory. Galicia was incorporated into the Polish General Government; Hungary received Carpatho-Ukraine in return for its services to Nazi Germany; and Rumania received Bukovina and Transnistria for the same reasons. Out of the remaining parts of the Ukraine the Germans formed the colony *Reichskommissariat* Ukraine.

The OUN then went underground to continue its fight against the German invaders. As a result, the Ukraine became covered with insurgent military units which, in October, 1942, united to form the Ukrainian Insurgent Army (UPA), commanded by Gen. Roman Shukhevych (Taras Chuprynka). Thus, side by side with the political struggle against the Nazis led by the OUN which the Germans called the *"Bandera-Bewegund"*, from the very beginning of the Ger-

222

man occupation an armed military struggle was also fought by the officers and men of the Ukrainian Insurgent Army (UPA). During this struggle, the Chief of the German SA, Victor Lutze, was killed in May, 1943, in the Kovel-Brest district of Volhynia.

The Nazi reaction to the active resistance of the Ukrainian people took various forms depending on the particular political situation. However, unscrupulous terror was continuously practised against the UPA. For instance, wounded members of the UPA who fell into the hands of the Germans were either shot or publicly hanged. The same unscrupulous terror was employed against the OUN-B on the territory of the *Reichskommissariat* Ukraine. On November 25, 1941, the headquarters of the Reich Security forces issued the following order to the special units of the SD:

> "Einsatzkommando S/5 of the Security Service and the SD. November 25, 1941. Headquarters. Daily Order No.12432/41, G.R.S.
>
> To the following bases: Kiev, Dnipropetrovsk, Mykolayiv, Rivne, Zhytomyr, Vinnytsa.
>
> Regarding: The Organization of Bandera.
>
> "It has been proved beyond all doubt that the organization of Bandera is preparing an uprising in the *Reichskommissariat* Ukraine with the aim of establishing an independent Ukrainian state. All members of Bandera's organization have to be arrested and after rigorous interrogation are to be liquidated in secret under the pretext of pillaging.
>
> Reports of the interrogations should be sent to the Einsatzkommando S/5."
>
> Erwin Schklitz,
SS-Obersturmbannführer.

According to this order, all members of the Bandera-Bewegund, that is of the OUN-B, arrested on the territory of the *Reichskommissariat* were tortured by the SD during interrogation and then secretly shot. These people, the "Banderites" members of the OUN-B — who fell into the hands of the

Gestapo, were the first victims of the "graveyard of the unknown" at Babyn Yar, near Kiev.

In Galicia which became part of the Polish General Government, the same methods, as were previously implemented against the Poles, were also put into practice against members of the OUN-B. Some of those arrested were shot. The rest were sent to concentration camps to face a slow death. Members of the OUN, arrested on the territory of Germany and Czechoslovakia, were treated in the same way. That is why Ukrainians who resisted the German occupants in Western Ukraine and were arrested, ended up in Nazi concentration camps. They were mostly people from Galicia, with only a few exceptions of people from Eastern Ukraine.

This is a brief explanation as to why Ukrainians were in Nazi concentration camps and why they were, on the whole, Ukrainians from Galicia. How many of them were there, and how many Ukrainian victims of Nazi terror were there altogether?

It is impossible to give a precise figure for this because the Germans did not keep accurate records of the exterminations. For example, after the war the Jews studied all the documents on the extermination of Jews and immediately accepted the figure 6 million as the total number of Jews killed by the Nazis. However, the Jewish researcher, Raul Hilberg in the appendix to his work *Destruction of the European Jews* entitled "Statistics on Jewish Dead" gives the figure 5,100,000. Others have stated that the number of Jews exterminated was only 4 million.

It is even more difficult to estimate accurately the number of Ukrainian victims of Nazism, for, as I mentioned in my memoirs, Ukrainian political prisoners were registered as Poles, Russians, Czechs or Hungarians, but not as Ukrainains. They were forbidden to wear the letter "U" as a description of their nationality. Therefore, it is impossible to estimate the number of Ukrainian prisoners in Nazi concentration camps.

The total of all Ukrainians killed by the Nazis lies between 3 and 6 million. The majority of these were Ukrainians serving in the Red Army who refused to defend the USSR and surrendered to the Germans. According to Hitler's instructions about 2 million of them were deliberately starved to death in the prisoner of war camps. In addition, no less than 1 million Ukrainians died as a result of "retaliatory actions" during which Nazi police and military units burnt down whole Ukrainian villages and killed all the inhabitants in retaliation for actions of the UPA and OUN. Tens of thousands of hostages were publicly hanged. Thus, in total, the Nazi occupants of the Ukraine murdered between 3 and 6 million Ukrainians.

P.M.

*

This book has been published with the financial help of Mr. and Mrs. M.M.B., USA, to whom the publishers wish to extend their sincerest thanks.